Statism Sucks! Ver. 2.0

Statism Sucks! Ver. 2.0

Andrew Ian Dodge

Authors Choice Press

San Jose New York Lincoln Shanghai

Statism Sucks! Ver. 2.0

Authors Choice Press
an imprint of iUniverse.com, Inc.

For information address:
iUniverse.com, Inc.
5220 S 16th, Ste. 200
Lincoln, NE 68512
www.iuniverse.com

cover © 2000 LIBA Design

Previously published in paperback by Blue Enterprises, Inc.
Media Division, Box 1070 Church Street, Weld, ME 04901 (207) 585-2299
ISMB 0-9678127-0-4

ISBN: 0-595-15254-6

Printed in the United States of America

Foreword

A Treatise on Freedom

Senator Rod Grams (Rep), Minnesota penned this little ditty in tribute to the last July 4th of the century. Perchance might the election of an independent Governor with a strong libertarian streak, in his home state, cause him pause for thought?

You cannot see it, but you will know instantly when it's gone

You cannot feel it, but it shelters you like a robe

You cannot taste it, but a taste was never sweeter

You cannot hear it, but it rings out like a thousand bells

You cannot buy it, though it often comes at a heavy cost

You cannot sell it, for it is not yours to sell

You cannot crush it, yet few things are more fragile

You cannot extinguish it, the flame will rekindle

You cannot keep it for yourself, it gathers strength when shared

You cannot force it upon another, that is not its nature

And while it can be stolen from someone without their consent,

Most of history's great battles have been waged to win it back.[i]

Acknowledgements

I would like to thank all those who have helped me with this book. From the editing of Robert Mallows, to the fine banners and sage advice of the mystical Jessica Eckstein, and to Elizabeth Locke Dodge, my mother and publicist: thank you. I would be amiss if I did not thank the man who started this whole thing rolling, Dwight Lanning, who first took a chance on me.

For their faith in my critical writing, I would like to thank Kurt Torster, Robert Edvardsson and Alex Summersby. Ditto, all those on GameRanger who helped keep me and my Mac running on the straight and narrow, especially Peter Cohen, Aaron Small, Julian Taylor, Thomas Gurley, Scott Kevill and John Bousfield. Philippe Bonneau, webmaster extraordinaire, needs a nod here as well as Dee Dee Benkie, Sean Moronski, Mike Beyham and all the other YRs who have been so welcoming and helpful to me.

My special thanks go to Vera, my canine inspiration.

Introduction

'Tis the dawning of a new age, one way or the other. To Christians, it is the dawning of the new century and the end of a millennium. To politicians of all colours and hues it is the beginning of yet another campaign cycle, the one which decides who will lead these United States and the world into the 21st century. It is the end of the American century and the beginning of an untitled one.

One group of people does not share the politicians' and pundits' enthusiasm for the next cycle. That is the most important group in this field of endeavor: the voting public. If trends are correct the year 2000 will see a record low turnout at the polls, more people will not bother to cast their vote, spurning their hard-won right to elect a President. Yet again, will we hear in the post-election analysis of the record low turnout for the youngest voters, and yet again we will hear why this occurred.

As this 2000 cycle begins, politicians of all parties with their advisors will be dreaming up new and innovative ways of patronising the young. Figuring out the best way of telling young adults ("young people" in their parlance) what issues should concern them, and not bothering to listen to what the young really care about. Why? Well it seems patently clear to one who is still part of that group, that the young simply believe "politics sucks" and all politicians are crooks.

Moreover, they believe that they will never see a penny in Social Security or Medicare. Despite this, politicians continue to tell them how they are saving both programs. Not many under 40 believe that there is any way to save these programs. Politicians promise to cut taxes and then figure out a way of raising them so no one knows what is going on. How can politicians be so stupid, so naïve, to think anyone with a brain will buy what they say. It is because they have forgotten what it is like to be young. They have forgotten or chosen to ignore the fact that most young adults are much better informed than politicians would care to believe.

Younger citizens' access to information through the media and the Internet is unprecedented in any age. They are more educated and better communicators than ever. And, most worrying to politicians, they have learned to think for themselves despite being force-fed by the media and academics. In short, scratch many a young adult and you will find a libertarian. They themselves often do not realise this, but slowly come to see their libertarian bent as they get older.

The purpose of this "treatise" is to express ideas and thoughts that millions of under-40's believe and to put a label on them. In the end, I wish the reader to say: "but I already know that." "This is the way I think myself." I seek to assist readers in clarifying their own political philosophies. Voters will be informed by their philosophy on Election Day and ready to vote. Then, watch out, you "business-as-usual politicians" of all parties.

Andrew Ian Dodge
August 2000

Contents

1

Personal Responsibility

Jesse Ventura, the ex-wrestler Governor of Minnesota is known for his forthright pronouncements. His feelings on personal responsibility are no different. In a recent meeting in his State, he was confronted by an unwed mother who insisted the state should pay for her child-care. In response, the Governor asked the girl why she thought the state had to pay for her bad decisions. It was a statement that stunned the nation and got the Governor a great deal of "bad press."

Why? Was Mr Ventura not expressing the feelings of a great many taxpayers in both his State and all over the U.S.? Where does it say in the Constitution that taxpayers have to pay for every mistake made by other individuals in their lives? Why is it that some expect the state to pick up the tab when a young woman gets herself pregnant, either by paying for an abortion or supporting that child until the age of 18? It is this sort of hand-holding by the state that has led both young and old to abandon any sense of responsibility, either to themselves or to their relatives. Why is it that older men and women complain that they are not getting enough to live on from Social Security? In the words of David Boaz, of the Heritage Institute, in his excellent "Libertarianism, A Primer": "Social Security not only took away the need to save for one's own retirement but weakened family bonds by reducing parents' reliance on their children (p. 142)." To this he adds, " the big problem is that as with any government program, Social Security's designers did not have to think about the future and weren't required to make their program financially sound (p. 222)."ii

In many families, patently unsound financial decisions are made to reduce assets. This of course, is due in part to the criminal inheritance and death taxes anyone with more than limited assets suffers, when wishing to pass on something to children at death. There is a belief that the government will bail you out later if you choose to squander your earnings when you are young. This is partly due to the fact that nursing homes gouge those who can pay at a high rate because they know that when the money runs out, the government will pick up the bill. In fact, because the government pays nursing homes less than they should for dependent patients, individuals are charged at a higher rate partly to compensate for government's low payments. Little wonder that most under 40 believe that they will see none of the money that they are paying to Social Security.

The "baby boomer generation," of which our embattled President is a part, are an odd and troubling problem. Because they had no self-control in their youth in the 1960's, now, as demonstrated by President Clinton, they assume that no young adults have any self-control or common sense. This generation, which now is in a position of power, is the personification of the phrase, "do as I say, not as I do." It is amazing that some of the most zealous participants in the sixties drug culture are now keen agitators in the "war on drugs." President Clinton admitted smoking pot on MTV during the '92 Presidential campaign. It would seem unlikely that Vice President Gore did not at least try drugs during his youth in the drug addled 1960's. Yet neither of these two powerful politicians, nor any of their boomer supporters, has ever suggested that cannabis should be legalised, even going as far as to express dismay in the efforts to allow "medical marijuana" in certain states.

Boomers have become the "neo-puritans" in the 1990's, seeking to ban anything that they deem "harmful." It is as if the drugs that were taken in the 60s and 70s have caused an entire generation to suffer group amnesia. Surely one of the benefits of the 60s revolution was the enhancement of rights of the individual over his own affairs. Bizarre as it may seem, there are more drug legalisation rumblings in the Republican Party than in the Democratic Party. Recently, Gary Johnson the conservative Republican Governor of New Mexico, while admitting that drugs are a bad thing and should not be taken, also admitted that the war on drugs is "a miserable failure." He stated that he believes that he is not alone in believing: "I don't think people should go to jail for smoking marijuana." Of course President Clinton's Drug Czar, Barry McCaffery, responded that the statements were "truly nutty." [iii]

A few days later, Jeff "Skunk" Baxter, a former Steely Dan and Doobie Brothers guitarist, made it public that he is thinking of a run for Congress in 2000, as a Republican. When challenged about his sex, drugs and rock & roll background he said, "I'm going to admit that I did all that stuff, but the most important thing is to learn from your past." He made it clear that any obfuscation of his past would just make it more interesting.[iv] If he should win, it will be interesting see the perspective Mr. Baxter brings to the House.

A wag of the left once suggested a possible reason that there is not more overt support for drug legalisation. It would adversely affect earnings of many of the constituents of certain key Democrats from large urban areas and maybe even certain politicians themselves. This may in fact, be an incredible jab at inner city politicians, but these self-same proponents of all sorts of "rights" never seem to include any sort of drug in their campaign. Indeed, these Representatives and Senators are often the leading advocates of the anti-tobacco suits being brought in the nation's courts. It's thus no surprise to see these same people jumping on the "anti-gun suits and bans" bandwagon. What may be closer to the truth is the likelihood that in fact earnings from illegal drug activities find their way into the coffers of politicians of all ilks and ideology.

The "neo-puritans" do not confine their activism to drugs and guns. These self-same participants in the "sexual revolution" are those now most keen to take any sexual element out of every day life, by pushing for draconian sexual harassment legislation. These born again-prudes are the first to suggest that a television program may have "unsuitable scenes" which could be as little as a brief glimpse of a nipple through a white blouse.

Hypocrisy, pervades the baby-boomer generation as well, in the form of feminists who crucify ordinary men for any slightly sexual remark and then allow an accused rapist and known philanderer for a President to get off scot-free for his lewd and lascivious behavior. Men have been fired from major companies and suspended from universities for jokes of barely discernible sexual content told around some woman who "offends" easily. While attempting to cull all forms of harassment (imaginary or real) from the work place and school, the politicians take millions of dollars from Hollywood; the industry that makes almost of all its money from the portrayal of sex and violence in movies, print and music. These women who are so concerned for their fellow "sisters", routinely give money and support to a party which actively seeks the money and company of arch hard-core pornographers, such as Larry Flynt, the publisher of the pornographic magazine: Hustler. Rape is a terrible thing, but by making every man out to be a "potential rapist", as young girls are told as they enter American universities, these feminists cheapen the event and distract from those who really are attacked and raped.

Young adults are no better, especially those who have grown up on public assistance. Because the system is so centralised and anonymous, teenagers no longer have to suffer the embarrassment of admitting they are pregnant. In some cases, a teenage girl who gets herself pregnant is better off than one who is not. She is able to get public housing faster and has less trouble getting public assistance. Children, to many inner city youth, are not a source of shame but a source of income. A child is not the only result; sexually transmitted disease and drug abuse are rife among this element. Should the girl come down with AIDS or any other STD, she and her child will become even more of burden to the state.

Social workers, believing all men to be violent beasts, rarely pursue the father, so as not to traumatise the young mother. Surely this course of action traumatises the already over burdened taxpayer by picking up the financial paternal responsibilities and lets the father off free to produce more unwanted children. Why aren't social workers or other officials of the state zealously pursuing the culprits and forcing them to take responsibility for their actions? And when they do pursue the father, does the race of the father affect intensity of the pursuit?

Fundamentally, the main problem is that citizens no longer believe in the precept that for every negative action there is a negative reaction (or consequence). They are so used to the thought that the state will take care of them, consequences become an afterthought through the parental activities of the government.

There is in addition to the belief in no-fault living for themselves, the belief that everything is always someone else's fault. Armies of lawyers filing frivolous lawsuits on behalf of clients, who clearly should have known better, do not help this. For example, there's the apocryphal story about the person who used Windex on his contacts which damaged his eyes when he wore them. He sued the manufacturer causing the company to post a warning label on every bottle informing customers of the danger of this practice. Surely this would be obvious to anyone who has the slightest bit of common sense. It is impossible to warn people against every possible stupid idea they may have. The human mind is capable of amazing feats of stupidity. No company consumer relations department will ever be able to think up every possible dumb idea their potential customer could think of, even if it were to occupy all of its time with the task.

High profile cases against big tobacco and more recently gun manufacturers are a further symptom of this "no fault" society. Surely common sense says that smoking three packs of cigarettes every day for 30
years might bad for you? Is anything in that great amount good for you?
How can a city sue gun manufacturers for deaths caused by young men
who have illegally acquired and used guns to commit murders? Surely it
is the fault of those who perpetrated the crime rather than those who
manufactured the devices used. Are we soon to see suits against auto-
mobile manufacturers for cars used in drunk driving deaths? When will
individuals start taking responsibility for their own actions? In the case
of the guns, there are those who wish to use the state to take away our
access to anything that we might use to hurt ourselves or others. Hence
the current campaign to ban guns, despite the fact that this is clearly
unconstitutional. Do we remember why the right to bear arms was
intentionally added to the Constitution of the United States?

In an interesting twist to the anti-tobacco campaigning of the
Federal government, they have now turned their attention to cigars.
However, there is a distinct lack of data about the harm that cigars do to
the human body. Never mind. Instead of waiting for studies to prove
their case, the National Cancer Institute released a study that stated that
"the health risks of occasional cigar smokers…are not known," adding
to this the fact that 75% of all cigar smokers are occasional smokers.
Cigar smokers are less likely to get lung cancer, coronary heart disease
and heart disease. Despite this study the NCI continues to push its
statement that "cigars are not a safe alternative to cigarettes." They consider the rise in cigar smoking "disturbing" and "alarming," and make
no attempt to correct the many inaccurate headlines in the media such
as UPI's "New Findings give more weight to warnings that cigars can be
at least as hazardous as cigarettes."[v] It is possible to see an anti-elitist
element to the new found campaign against cigars. Cigars are seen by
many as the smoke of the well-off, as comparable to cigarettes.

Because no one is responsible for his or her actions in the eyes of the state, we believe that anyone can be reintroduced into society. It is this sort of belief perpetrated by social workers that allows convicted paedophiles and murderers to walk free after serving part of their sentences. Perversely, law abiding citizens are persecuted under "Megan's Law," aimed at paedophiles for such isolated incidents as urinating off one's own front porch. And no one in the eyes of the law is permanently sick or unable to be rehabilitated. A possible solution is making social workers personally and criminally liable if any of their "clients" commit serious crimes again. Social workers currently carry liability coverage to protect themselves financially if sued after a "client" re-offends. Prisoners are now suing the state for allowing them to leave their sentences early and kill again. Murderers are allowed to go free, after pleading mental insanity, arguing with aid of a psychologist that voices (generally "the devil") caused them to kill and maim. In some sense, we are returning to a time of superstition where the cause for anything bad is evil spirits and "devil made him do it," is used to account for, and excuse, any evil action.

Man is perfectly capable of evil without the influence of an outside power. Of course, this scape-goating of the devil allows prisoners to be believed when they "become born again" or convert to one or another major religion. This conversion to the side of good is used in appeals for clemency and early release. It worries me greatly to see a well-meaning member of the clergy providing a good reference for some loathsome criminal at his parole hearing. The testimony should perhaps bear the warning label that a "man of god" will not speak ill of another human. Failing that, it might be a good idea to make clergy who speak on behalf of a felon, liable for any future crimes they might commit, as has been suggested for social workers. Who is to say that the devil or whatever other evil is at fault might not reintroduce himself into the brain of the convict? Surely such a powerful evil can overcome a recent convert to the side of good? This presumes the belief that religion is always a good influence; a belief not always borne out by history.

For those who are not possessed, there is the excuse of addiction or "substance abuse", as it is now called. Much like the "demon drink" of the Temperance Movement and the "reefer madness" hysteria (which was used to help criminalise the drug, marijuana) earlier in the century, criminals are being given lighter sentences if they undergo a course of treatment. Never once does anyone question that the individual chooses to exercise his free will, to drink himself into a stupor or inject himself with that first spoon of heroin. We are expected to believe the drugs attacked the individual and possessed him. We must make an exception for hospital addicts, like Soldiers in the Crimea, who were given heroin as a "non-addictive" pain killer. Hence the antiquated description of heroin addiction as "soldier's disease."

College campuses participate in this hysteria as well. When one student gets drunk and falls out of a window or a group of frat brothers get in a fight, the college administration immediately bans or severely limits alcohol consumption for all. Instead of prosecuting or disciplining the individuals involved, the entire community has to suffer for the actions of a few. Recently, Bowdoin took mass discipline to new heights, by using the drinking death of a visiting student as the precipitating excuse to ban all fraternities at this venerable college in Brunswick, Maine. This course of action is most prevalent in treatment of the young, about which I will write in a later chapter. However adult citizens are now being treated this way as well. Nation-wide seat-belt laws and the speed limits, recently re-introduced in the west of the U.S., are just some examples of this.

We need to take back our personal responsibility from the state and prevent the state from taking our responsibilities from us bit by bit. Sooner or later if this trend continues, the state will start making even more decisions for individuals. If the left succeeds in creating a National Health Service to cover all citizens in the U.S. It will begin to act like HMO's, dictating how adult men and women should be able to lead their own lives. With private health care, if one feels that a company is being too manipulating and intrusive, one may leave and go to another company more suited to one's needs. If the state is in control of this, there may no longer be as many private health plans and choices will be limited.

Part of personal responsibility is letting individuals see the consequences of their actions by allowing those consequences to have effect. If all forms of public assistance were at the lowest amount possible then people would be less likely to want to put themselves through the humiliation of asking for help. These individuals would be less likely to pursue any ill-advised course of action. Shame is a powerful weapon that forces individuals to examine their behavior and its possible consequences.

Personal responsibility needs to be taught to the youngest citizens and actively pushed throughout the educational system. It should not be the state's responsibility to bail out those who have made bad choices in their lives due to inattention or to ignorance. The state is there to provide them with the opportunity to pursue happiness; the state is not there to provide a "fail safe" for its citizens.

People should not be required by law to wear seatbelts, or to wear helmets on motorcycles, just as we should not stop anyone who wishes to skydive. If these people wish to risk killing themselves and help in reducing the stupid gene pool, then it should be no one's right or obligation to stop them from doing so.

In the words of Neil Innes on Monty Python's Live at Drury Lane, "How sweet to be an Idiot…"[vi]

2

Parents' Responsibility

There has been much discussion lately regarding the issue of parental responsibility and how much is being shown by the latest batch of parents in the U.S. The press and experts seem to agree that parents in the 90's are getting fairly poor marks for their behaviour. In essence, they are not actually exhibiting responsible habits, preferring to leave most of the task of raising children to the state via the schools, television and day care. These absentee parents blame the schools, as well as television and day care, when their children go out of control. In short, some parents believe children to be no more than a "lifestyle accessory" that, like a car, is to taken care of by someone else.

Children should be considered an expensive investment, like a new house or a yacht, not like a new car. It is estimated that it costs $112,000 to raise a child to 18 in the later part of the 20th century.[vii] Of course this does not include the cost of private school or college if parents want their child to have a better education. Children are also an investment in time and emotion. Raising children is not an easy task, in any era despite the many articles which tell parents how much harder they have it than did their parents or grandparents. It is rare in the U.S. that parents have a difficult time feeding their children, or keeping them from getting killed in a war or sickened by disease. Each generation has it easier than the previous one in the U.S. However, that is not to say that child rearing is easy, especially with the intrusiveness of the state, via social workers and counsellors. The choice to have children must be made under the right circumstances and with the right amount of forethought and planning, if possible. While so-called "accidents" do happen, there are plenty of ways now to reduce the possibility of pregnancy or in the case of various surgical procedures, eliminate pregnancy entirely.

The first question one must ask is, should these parents be having children in the first place? In the modern age, children are seen to be a right or a choice, but not many seem willing to accept the attendant responsibilities with that right. In pursuit of this right, parents of whatever age pursue the goal of having children "cost-be damned". With the advent of modern technology there are a myriad of ways that an infertile couple can have children, no matter what the age of the parents. From in-vitro fertilisation to surrogate mothers, childless couples are using all that this modern age can provide to acquire the elusive child.

Yet at the same time, younger women abort foetuses at an alarming but thankfully decreasing rate. If a pregnancy is not convenient for the potential mother she is more than willing to toss it away as if it were an unwanted garment. At the same time, potential adoptive parents are waiting for babies, some having to take the costly and risky step of adopting from abroad.

Add to this mix, politically correct social workers who do not allow children into homes that are not of the same racial or religious background, even if the child would be better off in a real home. One wonders what happens to children of mixed background. Who determines the racial type or religious background of the child? In some cases, it would come down the percentage of racial type in a truly "Heinz 57" child. This already occurs in the cases of aboriginal children, where they are placed according to their racial percentages. It is easy to see that the system is profoundly twisted. *A child is just a child.*

Each child needs a secure permanent home with at least one loving and responsible parent.

Many parents who have children in the 90's should not have a pet, much less a child. They are unable or unwilling to show any responsibility, other than financial (in most cases). They pawn the child off to day care as soon as they reach the minimum age required and using the TV, the Internet and gaming consoles to provide their children with company and companionship. These parents show no interest in their child's development, teaching them nothing except greed and envy. Men and women are more concerned with "having it all" than raising their children to be assets to the community. There is nothing wrong with ambition; it does great things for the country. But we must convince these sorts of parents to remain childless and allow themselves to contribute to the community in other ways instead of spawning neglected youths, potential criminals, state wards or mentally ill.

More and more couples are being counselled before they get married. Why are there no counsellors to talk to potential parents to see if they are truly committed to the task which they are about undertake. Institutions of faith are failing in this area as much as the parents. In accepting the changes that technology has brought to modern life, they have abdicated their role in the raising of the children of their communities. Instead of encouraging adults and their children into their churches, many of these institutions drive them away with their trendy services and politically charged ministers. When called on this fact, many churches complain that the "young" are no longer interested in church. This is instead of asking themselves why the young have been driven away from church and other faith based institutions. Moreover, since marriage often leads to procreation and raising children who need a good home and proper guidance, where is the counselling and support to come from, if not from religious institutions?

It is not politically correct to question the right of couples and even singles to have children. Any criticism of the fact is immediately tarnished as being mean-spirited and unsympathetic. As illustrated in the previous chapter, the fundamental problem is that no one believes there is a need for personal responsibility. If errant fathers and mothers were more apt to be pursued for child support, fewer would fly the nest. Recent aggressive government measures to pursue parents for child support may result in lower divorce and abandonment rates. Common sense suggests that any child will be better off with two loving and protective parents than with only one, even assuming that the one parent is a paragon of parental values and responsibility.

It is deemed unethical by the left, feminists and religious institutions to do anything to discourage adults from having children regardless of whether they are financially or mentally ready to do so. It is a problem when men and women who have barely grown up themselves, have children. These parents, encouraged to be their teenager's "best friend," spend more time trying to be liked than raising their children. A child does not need a friend when growing up, but does need guidance through the difficulty that is adolescence. Some theorists hold that the first five years of a child's life determine future behaviour, after that the "die is cast." In many ways, another die is cast atop the first during adolescence.

Alas, this sort of responsibility is not being instilled by the state and it will never be. It is not the state's responsibility to legislate morality. It is up to the community to encourage its citizens who are parents to take responsibility for their children and not expect others to care for them. One solution to this problem would be charging parents along with children when their children commit a crime. A variation on this procedure is being tried in some communities and states. Many parents would not welcome the thought of spending a night in jail when their teenager is caught vandalising property. In addition, parents should be financially responsible for the actions of their offspring, even to the extent of fining the parents as well as the child. If this sort of policy were put into action nation-wide, this would certainly focus the attention of parents and make sure they knew what their offspring were up to. It is well documented that many children who commit crimes do so for the attention of a parent. A parent should not be able to throw up his or her hands and say "I can do nothing," and then expect taxpayers to care for that child. This is in effect the principle of the emancipated minor.

As we enter the new century, parents must make an effort to understand the enormity of the task they are undertaking. The nation has never needed every married couple to have a large number of children to successfully pursue its goals. In fact, one could argue quite the opposite: if we as a nation continue to produce amoral, uneducated, ignorant and emotionally handicapped adults, we are doomed in the next millennium. Those countries that feel that their greatest asset is that their citizens will surpass us. American children are the most spoiled of any nationality in the world. Despite all they have, they continue to test poorly in aptitude tests on an international level and moreover, these scores are falling. It is no wonder that Silicon Valley must go to the Indian sub-continent and Asia to find highly skilled and dedicated programmers to do the coding used for modern computer programs.[viii] Parents in this country and schools shirk their responsibilities to the youth of America and are liable for a failing of a whole generation of children.

3

The Young

While education in its fullest sense will be discussed in a following chapter, in this section the young will be examined. The young are a troublesome area for American culture. We as a nation have no idea what to do with them and how to raise them. We continuously tell them that they are adults, but treat them as small children until they are 21. Even beyond that, we implore them to abstain from sex and drugs, but fill our popular culture with just those things. We schizophrenically patronise them, alternately calling them "young people" and children one minute to the next, depending on them whichever is more politically useful.

The expression "young people" really contains much of what is wrong with the way children are handled in the U.S. Why are they referred to as "young people" Young as opposed to what, young canines, young apes or is it young cats? "Young people" is taken to mean at various times, from age 10 to age 40. More often than not it is used as derogatory term, decrying the group's lack of interest in some or another aspect of life.

Why do we not use the term "young adults" for men and women between 16 and 40? Perhaps the problem is that no one knows how to define an adult. Do we define it when a young man or woman can marry, have a child, sign contracts, get a credit card, drive a car, own a gun or die for their country? Or are young men and women adults when they are allowed to drink alcohol? One of the greatest idiocies and affronts to freedom in the latter half of this century has been the national mandated raising of the age of drinking to 21.

The federal government behaved as it did with the moronic 55 miles per hour speed limit (there are far fewer accidents on highways with higher speeds allowed), blackmailing states into compliance under the threat of a curtailing of federal highway funds. Why should states need federal funds in the first place? It is their citizens' money that has been paid to Washington. Surely there should be no strings attached to any money that the federal government sends back to the states. Rather, the funds should not flow to the federal government at all. There will be more on the role of the federal government in a later chapter.

A man or woman may do a whole list of things before the age of 21, many of which have much worse consequences than having a drink. Surely if someone may enlist in the armed forces and die for his country, he should be able to have a beer without fear of prosecution. He is defending the nation for a freedom he himself is not allowed to enjoy. Why is it that a country, which bans alcohol until such a late age has one of the highest incidences of alcohol-related deaths and addiction in the western world? We give the young money in their pockets and credit cards, along with the freedom of the ability to drive. Is it not logical that they will not drive somewhere to have a drink? It is ludicrous to believe that teenagers with money in their pockets and personal transportation will not find a way of getting alcohol and going somewhere to drink it. Would it not be better to make the drinking age 18 so that men and women who are in college, a fairly protected environment, can experiment with alcohol and realise its limitations and dangers? Is it right that we deny someone who is working in a full time job, in many cases with a wife and children, access to a club or bar that is holding a rock concert? How can it be that we can give a 16 year old a licence to drive a high speed two ton piece of equipment made of steel and rubber that can cause multiple deaths and major destruction, yet he or she is not mature enough to have a drink?

Or would it be better still if we allowed families to teach their children at a younger age about alcohol, at the dinner table or with their friends? Surely we should demonstrate to teenagers how to have a drink and remain in control and respectable at the same time. It is my impression that where families have a drink together, children are more likely to learn responsible behaviour in this and other spheres.

In order to end the complication and duplicity of the situation, the solution should be to set a standard level of legal "adulthood." Whether it be 16 or 18 is a matter for others to decide. There are some that argue that with modern communications and education, we should lower the age of maturity to 12 or 14. Does it make sense that straight sex is legal between two young adults while two young adults of the same sex may not do something similar? Of course the fundamental point is that this issue would be best decided at the state level closer to the individual citizens.

As mentioned in another part of this work, the religious community is failing to address this issue as well. It seems that they feel that government knows best when it comes to raising the young. Scared into passivity by "civil" libertarians who take the 1st Amendment to the extreme, religious organisations seem to shy away from any guidance whatsoever for the young, except to parrot the statist pronouncements of "children's advocates." Rather than provide a positive role in children's lives to counter all that is bad, they ally themselves with neo-prudish censors who feel that if something is inappropriate for children then no one should be able to see or hear it anywhere. Churches and temples of all kinds should strongly make the case for what is right and what is wrong without reverting to tactics which make them appear an arm of the Nanny State. In study after study it has been found that children like certainty and order. They prefer things presented to them straight rather than in some mealy mouthed way that seeks not to offend them when discussing the facts and sound reasoning.

When discussing the young it is not long before we hear the debate about the influences of culture on their development or lack thereof. Usually this debate reaches a fever pitch after some sort of tragedy or outrage, leading to calls for draconian and hysterical legislation to protect "the children". It is interesting that one never hears a majority call for parents to do their jobs and take their responsibility for influences on their children from books, television, etc. The majority cry always calls on the government to do something.

With the advent of the Internet and proliferation of computers, the banners have yet another monster to slay. Video games, music and television are blamed for all young society's ills. Never once has anyone presented concrete evidence that a song, a TV program or a game has ever caused a child or young adult to commit a crime. Despite the lack of evidence and myriad of court cases that state the contrary, (violent lyric cases including suits against Ozzy Osbourne and Judas Priest) there are advocates who continually call for the banning and rating of such material. With the advent of the hype surrounding school shootings, computer game companies and moviemakers are now in the line of fire. Some of those targets include Id Interactive, creators of the computer games, Doom and Quake, Oliver Stone, director of Natural Born Killers and Scott Kalvert the director responsible for The Basketball Diaries.

Parents and educators of those who killed themselves or others or were killed look to assuage their loss and their guilt through financial settlements. In this they failed, at least they failed to win in court. We must all hope that there are sensible judges in these cases as there were with cases against metal and rap bands in the 80's. A great worry for anti-censorship types is fact that there is the possibility that the husband of a leading record and video burner of the 80's Tipper Gore, may be elected President in the year 2000. We could find we survived the arch-statist Hillary "State Health Care" Clinton only to be presented with a 21st century "Lord Protector" in the form of Tipper Gore. Will Tipper Gore be America's answer to Oliver Cromwell?

Children, if they are influenced by popular culture, would be better prepared to be able to make the correct decisions in life if parents, religious groups and educators did their job instead of whining about how hard it is to do. Most of all, it is incumbent on parents to raise the child they want to see go into society. This is not the role of the state. It is the role of those closest to the child and the individuals the children look to for guidance. Why must the entire nation suffer for errant and lazy parents who refuse to do what they have committed themselves to do when they started that child: guide and nurture the child into adult-hood?

4

Education

As of this writing, it has been over 6 months, since 13 teenagers died at Columbine High School in Colorado. The frenzy over this tragedy has not died down in any way shape or form. President Clinton and Congress are in a panic about what they can do in order to be seen to be doing something. Because guns were involved, the call has been to make buying and owning guns more difficult. This ineffective and idiotic response ignores the fact that 17 Federal and State laws were violated before and during the event. Furthermore, only 13 of the over 2000 cases involving guns taken to school were prosecuted. The truly cynical have something to chuckle about. If the two boys involved, had not had access to guns, as the explanation of the disaster in the high-school indicated, there is a good chance the death toll would have been *higher*! The two boys constructed over 40 bombs and had scattered them around liberally in the building. Some of these bombs consisted of propane tanks, fitted with timers and nails. If any of the larger bombs had gone off, the death toll would have been several times higher than 13. The boys planned to destroy the school in its entirety, with over 2000 students in the school. It is rather interesting that not much has been made of the fact that these boys were able to get all of their bombs into the school entirely undetected.

There has been a media frenzy against music, guns and the Internet, with an almost complete avoidance of the question of why these young boys were pushed to the edge and then over it. Only Fox news made any effort to interview the other members of the "Trench Coat Mafia." The Trench Coat Mafia were a group of children who felt themselves to be outcasts and geeks and hung out together to share common interests. Because of their mostly male membership and the occasional use of make-up, many of their fellow students considered them to be gay and said so, routinely. The name derives from the fact that many members of the group wore black trench coats to school over black clothing. In these interviews, we learned that the members of this group were verbally and physically abused on a daily basis by jocks. One of them reported that they were pelted with stones and bottles on a near daily basis. Where were the teachers and other school officials during all this? No doubt reporting this to any teacher earned the victims even worse abuse. The "in-touch" Principal was not aware of the group's existence, although most of the student body had known about them for two or more years.

The shooting perpetrators, Klebold and Harris, demonstrated time and again that they were a (psychological) mess, publicly via the Internet and in school, but nothing was done about it. The reason this issue has not been dealt with in a forthright way is that it would cause us to rethink the "Uber-jock", mentality in high schools and colleges. The term "uber-jock" was coined on Goth Internet newsgroups to describe the popular sports obsessed students who run many public schools in the U.S. The male students use both verbal and physical abuse to dominate many sectors in the school, treating the school as their own personal fiefdom. These "untouchables" are allowed to behave this way by teachers and administrators keen to stay popular with the right "crowd" of students. Our schools must be run for all students, not for the popularity of the teachers and "in" students.

The Littleton tragedy is just one of a host of school killing incidents, many of which go unreported as they occur in inner city schools, where it is almost "expected" by the media and general public. All of the high profile shootings share one distressing fact. No one knew it was going to happen. Despite the fact that these childrens' teachers are with them for 6 hours every day, these teachers never suspected a thing. More accurately, given the events we now are all familiar with, they were not looking.

A month to the day after Littleton, there was another school shooting. This time six were injured but none died. Because of the media frenzy involved in the Littleton case, there will be more and more of these events as desperate teenage boys take to copycat violence in a last desperate cry to be heard or seen. As might be expected, the calls for unconstitutional gun controls have continued to gather pace, with politicians from both sides of the aisle attempting to gain political capital as children are injured and dying. For those interested in more tales of torture and hate from the American High School system, there is an excellent site called "Tales from Hellmouth."[ix] The webmaster requires that all the cases of abuse be true. The site makes for some pretty depressing reading.

What has happened to our schools that have caused them to be in such a state? Public schools in the U.S. and U.K. have been ruined by one thing: the powerful teachers unions whose teachers practice politically correct teaching methods. There is no longer adequate discipline in public schools. It is not surprising then that American students routinely rank at the bottom of skills tables when tested against students from the rest of the developed world. Children are no longer learning; they are being indoctrinated in socialism and other left wing ideologies. It no longer matters whether or not a student can read and write. It matters more that they know how to behave in a politically correct manner.

After decades of attempts by Washington, D.C. and states alike to correct these acute problems, it has become obvious to all those who care to think for themselves that there is only one solution. We must privatise the public school system, and bring competition into the monopoly that the teachers unions have over our children. If a school cannot measure up, then its teachers should be fired and new ones brought in, while, also replacing incompetent curriculum administrators and rubber stamp school boards. Schools should have to compete for students. Private schooling companies should be able to bid to run the schools. If they fail to provide the proper level of service then another bidder will get the job. Thus, through a capitalistic evolutionary process, the level of education will rise. Kelly Services; a leading national supplier of temporary help is already providing substitute teachers for public and private schools nation-wide.[x]

The solution to this problem does not include draining more money from taxpayers. Even with the current sinking education level for the last 30 years, education spending has gone up while achievement has gone down. Is it that important to break the teachers' unions? After much resistance from the union, Massachusetts introduced teacher testing. Over 60% of the teachers failed to pass a test that contained basic skills needed for the job. Unfortunately the failing teachers were not summarily fired, as they should have been. A program of retraining has been put in place, spending even more of taxpayers money, to get these teachers to a reasonable level. Were scores changed and thresholds lowered in order to lower the number of teachers that could be considered incompetent?

Republicans and even some Democrats are in favour of school vouchers. Vouchers essentially give a tax rebate to the parent to permit them to spend their money for the school they think is best for their children. Parents are given a voucher for the amount the school system spends per child to help defray the cost of the private school selected. States with some form of voucher program include Florida (1999),

Milwaukee (1990) and Ohio (1995). There are court challenges to every such program. Cleveland, Ohio's program was suspended after a Federal Judge ruled it unconstitutional on the grounds that it violates the separation of church and state. The judge ruled that the program had the "primary effect of advancing religion" because a majority of the 56 private schools were religious. Over 4,000 students have been affected by this ruling, most from poor families. Several of the schools involved have reassured parents by telling them they will not turn away any student. It is clear that there will be an appeal. However it remains to be seen whether the students will be allowed to continue in their new schools during the appeal process. To make matters worse the challenge to the program is being funded and spearheaded by national groups like the Washington-based People For the American Way. This group and its fellow agitators are behind challenges to other voucher programs as well. [xi]

Never mind the fact that voucher programs are vigorously opposed by the left of the Democratic Party and the unions, they are simply too little, too late. There is seldom any suggestion that parents should not have to pay school taxes if their children go to a private school. Instead the proposal is to give parents back *their* own money to spend as they choose. Would it not be a better solution not to tax the parents in the first place and to allow them to spend their money on the level of education they desire for their child?

Many who defend the public school system and resist any moves towards privatisation or competition quote Thomas Jefferson in their defence. While he was a strong supporter of state funded education to instruct the populace in the difference between right and wrong, he would be appalled by what the school system has become. The most telling of quotes: "It is better to tolerate the rare instance of a parent refusing to let his child be educated than to shock the common feelings by forcible asportation and education of the infant against the will of the father."[xii]

Privatising the public schools could result in schools specialising, thus allowing students to be able to avoid going to "one size fits all" schools where the morons have to rub shoulders with the geniuses. These students could attend a school where the focus is on the mind, not the body. Spare us please, the ludicrous debates that occur in school boards across the country about whether to purchase sports equipment or new computers. Why should the parents of the non-athletes have to pay for jocks to be trained in a few sports to the exclusion of intellectual training for the good of all?

Another solution for the athletes' problem, is that athletics should no longer be offered at state funded schools, above and beyond physical education. The sports franchises and leagues could be encouraged to follow baseball's example in the farm team model. Another model could be the schoolboy soccer organisations of U.K. soccer teams. In fact this model has been used all over Europe to find and nurture young talent. In this system, young boys with talent are selected at a young age and nurtured by clubs from the time they are 11 until they are able to play professional sports. Then, once they are proficient, they either sign to the senior team or work their way up through the system via semi-professional teams and then through the three divisions to the Premier league. There are some similarities between this system and that of the farm-club system in baseball. However the soccer farm-clubs take in athletes much earlier than the baseball equivalents and do so while the student athletes continue in school.

Once students survive high school and manage to get into a good university, they face another set of challenges, most of which are not academically related. When a young adult enters most universities in the U.S., the PC (politically correct) machine and its system of indoctrination is ready to chew on the fresh mind. From day one of their new academic adventure students will be bombarded with messages that all the knowledge they arrived with is wrong and evil. White male students bear the most serious risk of bombardment, but those of a Christian faith can expect abuse and harassment both from their professors and their peers. They can expect their rights to free speech to be eliminated as well as the right of due process. In effect, when a white male enters university, his rights under the Bill of Rights cease. The best account of the perils of American universities can be found in the excellent *Shadow University* by Alan Charles Kors and Harvey A. Silvergate. [xiii]

We must separate the universities in the U.S. into two categories before we examine this point further. There are of course public (state) universities and private ones. Considering that most of the private universities receive federal monies, I will examine this granting of federal funds and the blackmail, which accompanies it, in another section of this document.

First and foremost, taxpayer funded universities should not breach the rights of any of its students in any way. Clearly all rights afforded to the average citizen exist for all students at a state-funded university. There should be no question that such abrogation of rights is illegal both under state and federal law.

Private universities on the other hand may treat their students in ways that would be contrary to law in a public setting. After all, private universities are private companies who are able to make rules as they see fit. However, should any of the universities receive any money from the federal government, then their rules and regulations come under the scrutiny of state and local authority. It is interesting that many of the more errant private colleges and universities only assert their "private" nature when defending some egregious breach of students rights under the Constitution and natural justice.

In one bizarre case, the School of Social Work at the University of Minnesota banned all fragrances from the department. The dictate, encompassing both the student and faculty, bans all colognes, perfumes and even some shampoos. The department plans to try to spread its ban so that all departments in the building it shares are also fragrance-free. The justification for this lunacy is that there is some evidence that a small minority of individuals suffer from "multiple chemical sensitivity environmental illness."[xiv] Before we chuckle at this stupidity it should be noted that the City of Halifax, Nova Scotia, has a similar ban in place in all public places and offices. And wouldn't it be interesting to know, first, does the new condition exist? And if so what percentage of 1% of the population are so afflicted? And is there even one so-affected person in the constituency of the institution? Is there no better way than to quash the actions of all for the benefit of (maybe) one?

Universities in the U.S. are producing badly educated and ignorant students who have been brainwashed by members of the 60's generation who pervade these schools of higher education. Those who attempt to retain their individuality and resist "training" are harassed and persecuted in such a way that not only affects academic records but employment prospects after graduation. Professors prefer pliant students who are more willing to jump through Pavlovian hoops than explore their educational independence. Those who do not know much are easier to brainwash into believing the "politically correct" way. Many a professor has been heard to say as one of mine did, "their brains are mush and we must mould them!" This emotional blackmail and at times, physical bullying, causes many students to simply "keep their heads down." Universities in the U.S. now resemble more a country behind the Iron Curtain than our country as described by the Constitution. Ironic isn't it, that the Iron Curtain has come down, but our universities have preserved the methods developed there. In most cases, professors and the administration either encourage such behaviour or do nothing about it when it occurs.

Those professors and administrators that speak up to defend students who are caught in a firestorm, finding themselves personally under fire and their own prospects of "tenure" and thus their continued employment at risk. Newspaper burnings, beatings and verbal harassment are commonplace for outcasts on many campuses. How soon before the tragedies befalling public high schools in the U.S., appear at the colleges all over the land? The author of this work knows of many people who have come close to this sort of action while under harassment at well-known liberal arts colleges. Is there any wonder that the rate of suicides continues to escalate year after year in the American higher education system? One college, U.C. Berkeley, has barred its tower windows because too many students were jumping out of them during finals week.

As with the public school system in the U.S., the best solution to this problem is the complete privatisation of all universities whether public or private. No federal or state money should be spent on these institutions. All the money should be raised either via tuition, corporate sponsorship or donations. The state and federal government have no business funding institutions that routinely and knowingly violate both state and federal law. If the Truth were told the State should not be funding secondary education at all, thus making them all private institutions. These will work to educate children whose parents choose the school and retain the tax-free status currently granted to private schools. However the requirements should be relaxed to ensure real freedom of education opportunity. Donors and parents will see that the institutions live up to their educational mandates.

The millennium is yet another example of the education system failing our children. No one seems to be able to correct the glaring error that sees the country celebrating 2000 years since the Birth of Christ a year early.

5

The State

In recent times there have been two cases that underline the challenge that exists in preventing the State from being totalitarian and which both pose great questions about how we should be governed. Although one of these two examples is occurring in the U.K., it is relevant to the U.S. The "left" in the U.S. looks to Britain and more importantly Europe for clues as to where they see that we should be heading in the next century.

In the north of England a man lay brain dead in the intensive care unit of a hospital. Some time before his death he had signed up to be an organ donor at his local post office. Of course, what the State did not know was that he instructed his relatives that there should be one caveat to the donation of his organs: that his organs should not go to any non-white recipients. Reluctantly the doctor in the ward agreed to this request and the organs were given to several needy patients.

Result: Since this incident was leaked to the press by an irate member of the local government union (UNISON) there has been an unrelenting row about the case. The organ donation agency, while agreeing that the request was distasteful, defended its action as it resulted in saving a life. They then pointed out that fewer organs were being donated than were needed. Critics have been unmoved and are calling for the law to be changed. The law as exists now, in England, stipulates that organ donation is a choice that is made by an individual before his or her death, with or without additional stipulations. [xv]

Those who are crying foul in this case insist the law should be changed so it agrees with laws in the rest of Europe. The law in most European countries is that all citizens are automatically organ donors unless they opt out of it. In short a citizen's organs are property of the state on loan to the individual while he needs them! The present Labour government has defended the U.K. organ donation agency and given strong indications that the law will not be changed, despite the protests from both ethnic minority organisations and the unions, Labour's usual political base.

As with the photo ID debate under the last U.K. government, the English tradition is less trusting of the government than some of their European neighbours. In many countries, such as France, it is mandatory that every person carry an ID at all times. In the U.K. one has 48 hours, after being asked to produce proof of identity by the Police, to do so. The need to instantly prove one's identity is anathema to the English common law tradition of being innocent until proven guilty. The use of identity cards is a necessary tool of the authoritarian state. They are against any tenet of a "free" society. In an extremely worrying development, some more authoritarian elements in the debate proposed that all cards be equipped with a chip so that they might be read by a scanner by police, if the card was available anywhere on the citizen's person and so without being shown by the card owner to the requesting official.

The second case is based in the U.S. and is all the more important in the light of the fact that Hillary Clinton is running for the U.S. Senate in New York. This is, of course, the question of a national health care system. Most other countries in the western world have such a system in one form or another. The two cases are related because many of the calls for the change in the law in the organ donor example referred to above came from U.K. National Health Service staff.

The British NHS suffers from an acute shortage of junior and senior Doctors. The pay and conditions are not sufficient to attract doctors into NHS. Many health authorities must import doctors from abroad to fill their needs. At a recent British Medical Association conference, junior doctors voted to take strike action in the coming year. Is this what Americans want, a system that can be held hostage by the unions, even at the expense of patients' lives?

One must also remember that most of the major medical discoveries in the last 40 years have occurred in the U.S. and more importantly, patients from other countries, many with a national health system, come to the U.S. and its private hospitals to receive treatment. Patients of other health systems come for one of two reasons: either the treatment is not available on the state system or the waiting list for the procedure is so long that the patient will be dead before he gets the needed operation. In the U.K., the NHS maintains a waiting list for waiting lists for some operations. So aware was the last Conservative government of this problem that they set about selling a large chunk of the NHS to private organisations and trusts. The current Labour government wishes to exercise more oversight of private healthcare, but does not look ready to reverse these initiatives. They too realise that a State cannot afford the social costs associated with complete cradle-to-grave medical services for a large population and that the State's methods may not be the best to accomplish the goal of public health improvements.

What many who support a national health system in the U.S. do not realise or care to admit, is that much of the cost of health care in the U.S. is not greed, but insurance cost caused by the multitude of lawsuits that occur every year. The U.S. does not need a national health service, its needs comprehensive tort law reform.

Recycling laws rank as some of the most disruptive and ineffectual example of the "Nanny State." Alas, there is probably no study on the effect of having to separate one's rubbish by law under the threat of heavy fines, on family relations. How many major family arguments are started by the incorrect placement of an item in the "regular" trash? Is there any proof that all the effort put into this process in time, gasoline (for the trucks to come pick up or the individual to take it to the "recycling centre") and manpower actually does anything for the environment? Surely all the gasoline wasted in getting the separated rubbish around offsets the savings in rubbish storage costs? Would it not be better to employ some of the unskilled labour in the U.S. to sift through the rubbish and separate those things that are recyclable? Is it helpful to the environment to have individuals burning their personal paper so that they are not put into a communal collection that is burned at a later date? Is it fair to make everyone buy a shredder to protect his or her privacy? Or is it helpful to make it so expensive to throw away some items that people dump and bury these items on their own land rather than pay a "dumping fee?" How long will it be before a pushy "recycling centre" employee is assaulted after accosting a resident over the contents of his rubbish bags? Surely, before long technology will exist to sort recoverable elements from waste after incineration, like glass, metal and plastic?

It is clear to most observers that both Federal and State governments in the U.S. are bloated monsters unable to care for even the basic needs of their citizens with the sole exception of defending it against outside threats. Alas, the defence funding is being cut. In the state of Maine, state government is the largest employer. Bath Iron Works, second only to the state in the size of its workforce, has a strong union. BIW is heavily dependent on defence contracts, however its unions are enthusiastic and sometime violent supporters of the Democrat Party, a party that routinely cuts defence spending when in power. The BIW union leadership has yet to make a link between advising its members to vote Democrat and the loss of jobs due to the ensuing defence cuts.

The State meddles in all sorts of affairs in which it doesn't belong, either according to the Constitution or for reasons of effectiveness. Why does the federal government feel it needs to fund the arts? Many on the social right of the Republican Party are against the National Endowment for the Arts because of what it funds, not because it funds the arts at all. When has the State ever supported great works of art? Private philanthropists have funded most of the greatest works in the West. The funding of art by the State is a socialist ideal, more commonly found in Nazi Germany and the Soviet Union. Why does the U.S. government need to buy up large tracks of private land, thus turning many rural states into giant parks that produce nothing for the local populace?

The federal government uses its vast resources to blackmail states into doing what it wishes at the local level. When indeed the federal government sends money to the states, it trumpets this action as Washington's beneficence in action, much as the European Union. It does not seem to matter to those who put up the self-congratulatory signs that this money is in fact the taxpayers' in the first place and not a gift.

In the town I live in, in Maine, there was a recent example of why communities should provide the help that is needed by individuals. In the spring, a local family of meagre means suffered a house fire and complete loss of their belongings. The community's reaction was instant and decisive. The day of the event there were tins for donations in local stores. A supper was quickly organised to raise money for the family and a place was found for them to stay. The family and their town are rebuilding their home. This is a clear example of why most things should be handled at the lowest level possible. State and federal government would have taken days if not weeks to accomplish some of the same without the all-important personal and friendly, level of care.

It has become clear that the main problem in the U.S. is that its national government has far too much money to spend. Despite this, the government resists any attempt to lower taxes. Federal and state government serves only to perpetuate bureaucracy, to feed the machine. There are scores of government employees who spend their time coming up with new and innovative ways to spend the taxpayers' money and thus to justify their existence when they are not in meetings and on training courses. Despite all the best efforts of President Ronald Reagan and to a lesser degree President George Bush, government grew under their tenures as much or more than it did under the Democrats. While some of this is due to the Democrats that dominated both Houses of Congress during that period, much is the result of that greatest of incentives for modern politicians: pork.

Pork is the weapon of bureaucracy to accustom constituents to the gravy train. For example, many voters will vote out a politician who has not brought them "their fair share." The state welfare system for the States is as addictive as welfare is for individuals, with states unable to free themselves from the lure of "free" money. There seems to be a collective amnesia about the fact that the citizens and businesses in these States paid the federal government money on tax day in April and all year round. Republican Senator Trent Lott, Majority Leader of a party who claims to be in favour of reduced government, is well known for his ability to bring pork to his home state of Mississippi.

There is but one solution to this problem: The U.S. must do away with its federal income tax system. Close business at the Internal Revenue Service. Create a whole new taxation scheme. Instead of individuals and companies paying taxes to the federal government, states will pay a "tithe" to Washington to cover the bare essentials of the nation (defence, central bank and currency, and basic commercial law). Each state will pay 15% of the their collected income tax to Washington. In hard times, total state incomes will likely fall, so the 15% payment to the federal government will be a smaller. This tax scheme will cover the obligation of all state citizens both corporate and individual. Each state will tax its citizens in the manner that their citizens select through the elected representatives. It could include a variety of taxes, income, sales, capital gains, corporate tax or a dependence on other tax raising methods. This tax regime does not include any estate or inheritance taxes or other levy on involuntary transfer of property as in the case of death. It is interesting to note several curious features of this scheme: the larger the total tax collected by the state the larger the payment of the state tax due to the federal government. Perhaps however, the state and its citizens will opt for lower total taxes to promote the local economy and, at the same time, reduce the payment the state would make to the federal government. Taken to the extreme in the many states, this scheme could result in a very significantly reduced federal budget.

A proposed state tax regime would be a flat percentage method. Individuals in each state will be charged a flat fee of 15% of their total income with no exceptions. Those couples with total income of under $40,000 and individuals with earnings less than $25,000 will be charged no tax at all. For example based on 1998, 62% of resident tax filers in the State of Maine would be exempt filing or paying taxes under this plan.[xvi]

Instead of promising to give more money back to the individual, the State will not take as much. There will be no need for tax cuts. It will then be in the best interest of the federal government that all states do well financially, so they get more revenue, likewise for the state. This should prevent the federal government from getting involved in areas of state and local affairs where they have no constitutional interest.

In the last 10 years there has been a worrying trend in government. It is not enough that the State taxes and regulates business with increasing complexity, now the government is competing against private companies. Added to this, the proliferation of non-profit corporations has been staggering in the last 5 years. The organisations tend to employ a whole myriad of lawyers and social scientists who produce nothing worthwhile for society. They spend on high salaries, the money earned by productive members of society and paid to the State via taxation. More worrying is that many of these organisations spend much of their time justifying their existence and budgets at the expense of their "stated" purpose.

In many cases these organisations provide services already available in the private sector undercutting private business in the process. State and Federal government, by allowing the private companies to be undermined, are actively and routinely hurting the economy. The most obvious example of this is prison labour contracted to provide goods and services at prices at which no private company can compete. It makes perfect sense to allow prisoners to learn a skill and make some money. It is reasonable that the state uses the prisoners to produce license plates as this has traditionally been a state function (although not necessarily so). However when prisoners make, for example: furniture, these prisoners compete against private business. The result is most undesirable. Think about it, you pay taxes for law enforcement to pay to get criminals off the streets, then the state turns around and uses those prisoners to bid against your company. You lose the contract thanks to a group who are supported by your own taxes. Did Jefferson intend any such situation? Not likely.

While politicians, prominently led by Pat Buchanan, complain about jobs being moved overseas at the cost of American workers, little or nothing has been said about the threat of home grown not-for-profit and government organisations undercutting viable private companies.

There is however a positive trend in the administering of prisons, that of private companies running them for the state under contract. This is an excellent trend which should be continued. The prisons are better run and more successful in their purpose. It is good to see prisons finally run for a profit after being such a leach on society for so many years. The men and women inside may not be doing anything positive for society but at least the privately run prison itself is less of a drain on the public purse.

If a private company does compete successfully against an arm of the government, then that arm attempts, and many time succeeds, in arguing for a law that protects its position. A case in point is the recent Postal Service regulation that requires the over 2 million private post box users who have post boxes at commercial companies such as Mailboxes Etc. to provide personal information that would be available to the public. This violates the Post Office's own privacy rules and opens the companies up to fraud. In addition, at a cost certain to hurt small businesses, the post box holder must inform all correspondents that suffix PMB must be added to all mail. If this is not on such correspondence after 24 October of this year, the mail will be returned to sender. [xvii]

The federal government and non-profits have become addicted to federal funding of their efforts. They force their work into the federal category spending, classified as "Entitlements." This spending which some in government believe is written in stone, expands exponentially every year. This is a deliberate attempt to make it more difficult to cut the budget and eliminate programs and is the main reason why cutting taxes is perceived as difficult. However, nothing is written in stone in Washington. It is possible to cut spending at all levels of government, the category of "entitlements" is not based in law but in Washington habit. It is because of this mentality that a proposed $792 million tax cut is considered extreme by some on both sides of the congressional aisle. In the same breath a politician praises his efforts to create a government surplus and then tries to explain to hard working Americans why they must continue paying high taxes. Some argue that the surplus is entirely a figment of Washington's collective imagination. For the sake of argument we will assume that this "surplus" does in fact exist. It would be amiss not to point out that the tax cut even at its highest level is not even close to the amount of the "surplus." According to the National Center for Policy Analysis's Bruce Bartlett, the surplus totals $2 trillion. Even with the tax cut, taxes are higher than they have ever been, currently 21.7% of GDP; averaging 20% during the Clinton Presidency. Taxes are higher than the average between WWII and the beginning of his two terms (19.2% in 1992). If you remove the collection of Social Security taxes, we actually have a $2 billion surplus this year. According to the Congressional Budget Office, unless there is a large tax cut, taxes will stay at the level of 21% of GDP. Even if taxpayers receive the maximum requested by the Republicans, it will not equal the amount of the tax rise in 1993 and will result in a small reduction in the projected *increase* in taxes over the next 10 years.

The usual explanation is that it is needed to be kept for a so-called rainy day. Only in government would this sort of perversity exist. Washington by having a surplus, has essentially overcharged taxpayers for its services. What other business would get away with keeping any excess payments you paid to them? To make matters worse, there are those in Washington who eagerly attempt to find a way to spend this surplus and avoiding giving it back to the taxpayers. The most useful of these excuses is to shore-up Social Security and Medicare. Never once do these politicians accept responsibility for the programs being short of money in the first place. To anyone outside the Beltway, the solution is clear: reduce tax rates immediately so less money will flow to Washington, thus working off the surplus. Let taxpayers use their own money. It's likely that the additional disposable income will be spent for goods and services that provide real jobs, or saved to produce investment funds.

It would be amiss to merely criticise individuals for their reliance on government. Corporations are as addicted to milk from the self same cash-cow. Corporate welfare statistics are staggering. If the payments and credits were ended tomorrow the government would be able to afford the Prescription-Drug benefit for Medicare, provide $250 billion for education and national defence and $500 billion in tax relief and debt reduction. [xviii]

That is of course if you believe this funding should go anywhere but to individual tax cuts. The only other needy projects in the list above are the chronically under-funded but over-stretched military and debt relief. By some estimates, the Federal government sends over $160 million to various powerful corporate entities. President Clinton has suggested that this colossal figure be increased by 10% for the next fiscal year. This is slightly above the current rate of increase over the past 4 years. [xix]

The public is only partly aware of this habit and even at their level of knowledge is overwhelmingly against it. There are no signs that the Federal Government will make any attempt to wean these corporations from the national teat.

With a privatised education system and no state funding of the arts or sports, the state will have enough funds to do the much needed infrastructure work on the roads and bridges. States may then decide if they can afford services such as welfare. If a state does not provide social services, then organisations that provided these services in the past, such as churches, local organisations, charity organisations and non-profits will be able to do these duties without the waste, fraud and mismanagement associated with state employees. A truly far-sighted state or town may well put its fire and police services out to tender to the private sector, thus inserting competition into previously monopolised services. As Lady Thatcher stated at the 1999 Conservative Party Conference, "the task of government is not to dominate people but to provide the framework for them to live their lives. [xx]

6

The Information Age

One of the most profound changes to life in the late 20th century is that of technology and its personalisation. Individuals now own more computing power than was dreamed of when computers were in their infancy 30 years ago. The Internet and e-mail have changed the face of how we as individuals communicate with each other. State monopoly post offices all over the world have been forced to change their services in order to stay viable. Communication now takes seconds rather than minutes or hours, and we are now seeing only a tiny part of what the silicon chip can do for humanity.

Soon anyone who wants to will send or receive e-mail and speak from anywhere in the world to anyone else anywhere in the world. What used to be the realm of governments is now available to all. With a Global Positioning Satellite navigation system it is possible to determine one's location on the globe within five feet. No longer do we need to ask for directions.

To lovers of freedom, the Internet is a gift from the gods. To a Statist, it's a cyberpunk nightmare come to life. It is now possible for a private person to send encrypted information so that no one, not even the government, can determine the content of the message. Not everyone is convinced of the sanctity of encryption and it is still unwise to consider it totally secure. Entire communities are being developed that are not under the oversight of any government body. Cyberspace is truly free. There are now even cyber-nations, which have declared themselves to be independent countries, free of taxation, or laws of any other given state.

The Internet lets individuals find work, get paid and live where they like, in some cases never physically meeting their employers. Collections of men and women now write software, develop technology and in some cases develop entire OS systems (i.e. Linux) never having actually met their co-workers.

True, this wild frontier aspect of total freedom leads to some abuse of that privilege, in other words a lack of the responsibility, which is the complement of freedom. It is true that there is large amount of pornography on the Internet and that a small percentage of businesses on the Internet are criminal. To many, this is a price worth paying. Criminals existed well before the Internet. Technology is finally the means to freedom that many have suspected it could be. The Internet is making a great effort to self-police itself, via the use of information networks (web pages, message boards and newsgroups) and traditional law enforcement.

With an ISP (Internet Service Provider), a telephone line and a computer any individual can publish anything for a potential audience of hundreds of millions of people. Young men (or predominately men) are running gaming sites that have more hits (number of online accesses) per day than the yearly circulation of even the most popular print magazines. These readers are frequently from every part of the world. On-line games now allow people from all over the world to meet and do battle with other people in cyberspace. Friendships are made between people who may never meet each other, across ethnic, racial, cultural, gender, religious and political boundaries, and defying even linguistic hurdles.

Now individuals from anywhere on earth with access to the "Net" may converse with people with similar interests, exchange ideas and compare notes. It is possible to find information on almost any subject at any time of the day or night in any time zone. More often than not this information is now available from several different sources. Of course young men have taken to this technology fast. Computer literate males now perfect their video game skills against the best in the world. Instead of relying on inferior Artificial Intelligence to provide a challenge, now they have fellow humans to play against. As a result it's now possible for those who excel at on-line multi-player games to earn money and prizes competing in organised matches via the Internet. Lest you think this is all violent first person shoot-em-ups, men and women can compete in games of every sort. It is now possible to get a chess game on-line any time of the day.

Via this technology it now possible for young men to become millionaires even before they are able to drive a car, or buy a drink. One no longer knows or cares the age of the person one is doing business with. That webmaster you deal with could be barely into high school. Proficiency finally counts more than age. There are a few laws, which still apply to transactions with minors, several of, which allow a minor more leeway in getting out of a business contract. Still any minor who abuses this privilege will soon see his web design business dry up.

Yet with all this opportunity, there are still those who strive to kill it. Statists from all over the world wish to regulate technology, denying their fellow citizens access to the opportunity that is the World Wide Web. A number of Statists wish to tax the transactions that occur on the net, not realising that this is not only a foolish strategy but technically impossible. Like a rapidly running river, the Internet will flow around any impediment. Web hosting can exist anywhere. It is a simple procedure to move a site from one location to another. Done correctly, it is possible to move an entire site, an entire business out of one jurisdiction into another, in less than half a day. The genie is out of the bottle and it cannot be corked, not by one or one hundred greedy politicians or bureaucrats.

With the Internet, traditional media has been usurped. No longer do we need to rely on the vagaries and prejudices of one or another major newspaper or magazine editor. On any given subject or event we can get a myriad of opinions and views. Instantly there are thousands of people discussing and analysing any given event that occurs world-wide, spreading the news through the web to anyone who wishes to see it.

Television news, formerly the main source of news for most Americans, is losing market share every year. The networks have been forced to show their TV output on the Internet. Any individual can watch news from anywhere in the world. Stories from one country are frequently broadcast by foreign news outlets and re-broadcast on the Internet. Now editors have to worry about being seen as weak or biased on the news, because if a newscaster does not run the story, someone somewhere else will. Worse yet for television, one of its core audiences, males 12-35 are deserting it in droves for the Internet for their frequent news fixes. Poll after poll on the Internet shows that males of this age group are more interested in playing a game online or surfing the net than passively accepting force-fed television. For those who do not have web access, television fare is getting worse. They may have more choices but quality is suffering as the networks, both cable and broadcast, aim their content at the majority of those left watching television.

The Internet is just one important aspect of the technology that frees individuals. Mobile phones and faster, cheaper transport augment this by providing the individual with fast geographical accessibility. An entrepreneur can run his business from anywhere on earth and perhaps soon, anywhere off-earth. All that he needs is a phone and a computer with the occasional low-fare plane ticket.

What does all this technology mean for freedom? Will there not be a new "have and have-not" category between the information rich and those who are information poor? Technology weakens the control of the State. This uncontrolled medium allows unlimited access to the world of knowledge. It means individuals are no longer tied to where their employers are based, and they may work from anywhere they wish. An individual with a good idea has an easier route to success. An idea, if it is good one, can spread throughout the world at a touch of a button. Within hours, an idea will be dissected and returned to its owner by web contacts with intelligent and erudite criticism. With encryption, even the most paranoid of governments will not be able to touch it. The downside being that with every leap in computing power a type of encryption weakens in strength. All this technology is truly the domain of the young. It moves so fast that those who wish to stop it have a hard time understanding what they are trying to stop. In order to stop hackers, companies must employ hackers. Hackers, a distinctly anarchist breed, spend much of their time making the secret open, and the hidden, obvious. It does not matter to a hacker if a large company or a government owns the site they wish to crack; it is all in the thrill of the deed.

The Internet is fundamentally a libertarian construct. Ironically, it was created by the U.S. government but soon thereafter took on a life of its own, as Internet II. The Internet will continue to empower those who choose to use it. Each person who joins it cuts away a tiny piece of the power of the State(s) regionally or nation-wide, world-wide especially.

What will the future bring? Well, several things are obvious. Computing power will continue to grow by leaps and bounds, allowing people to create virtual worlds on their desktops. With the advent of advanced phone systems it will be easier to communicate from any-where in the world. Soon it will be possible to have one phone number for any place you wish to be in the world. One will be able to carry one's mobile anywhere in the world. As the mobile power of the phones grow, so too will the access improve to the Internet from mobile phones. Soon, it will be possible to sit on the beach in Fiji and run your web-based business regardless of where the business is actually sited. Those nations that still have totalitarian regimes will find themselves even more isolated and besieged. Dissidents will be armed with small camcorders attached to a mobile phone broadcasting to an audience of millions. The freer states of the world will find it nigh on impossible to keep anything secret.

Soon, it will be possible for humans to have technology implanted in the body. Cyberpunk visions, currently the realm of science fiction writers and cutting edge doctors, will become common place. A malfunctioning organ replaced by a manufactured one, will allow those who are blind to see, without legs to walk and without arms to lift. Medical technology will continue to expand life expectancy well past the century mark. Governments and lawyers, always the slowest to react, will be faced with more problems looking after older people. Soon, mandatory retirement ages will be irrelevant, as people will be more than capable of working well past their seventies.

The populace will have better access to information and learning. They will be able to communicate more easily and quickly with one and another. They will be able to do business in ways no one ever thought possible; products will be released world-wide at the same time and be distributed to anywhere with a mail service. The world is changing rapidly, and we have no idea where it is going to end up. Will it be a better world? That remains to be seen. At least it will be an interesting ride.

7

Foreign Policy

Foreign policy has always been a difficult issue for libertarians. In truth, libertarians could be described as the ultimate peace-niks against war in all its guises, save for the defence or the integrity of the nation. In reality, life is not that simple. There are, no doubt, those who supported the war in Kosovo, and the Gulf War. In modern life it is sometimes hard to define what is in your country's interest and what is not.

The most difficult to defend of the two listed above is also the most recent. The war over Kosovo hailed by the left and the White House as a great victory is anything but a victory. The Kosovar campaign saw the transition of NATO from a defensive organisation to that of an offensive one. The war in Kosovo violated Articles 2, and 4 of the NATO Treaty[xxi], a fact that was entirely ignored by the White House. NATO, led by left of centre governments in the U.K. and U.S., led an aggressive war against a sovereign nation over a civil war inside the confines of its territory. Both President Clinton and Tony Blair, the British Prime Minister, were perfectly willing to use NATO ground troops to invade the Kosovar province of Serbia. Fortunately for both leaders, the air war convinced the Serbs to pull out of their own land. The actions are being hailed as a victory, but it is hard to see why. The Serbs managed to "ethnically cleanse" most of the Albanian population, only to be "ethnically cleansed" themselves by the Kosovo Liberation Army. The KLA is a drug-running, arms-peddling terrorist group bent on an independent Kosovo run by Albanian mobsters. The KLA came back from near obscurity thanks to NATO and its airforce. NATO has now decided that the former rebels will now form a new police/defence force for the province, even though, there is growing evidence that they have not disarmed as they agreed to do.

The justification for this conflict was the atrocities being committed by the Serbs in Kosovo. While appalling to any sane individual, these crimes are no worse than anything committed by either side over the long and bloody history of the area. The two leaders chose to ignore some key facts of the area, relying on the ignorance of our citizens to support their unjustifiable actions. Never did Clinton or Blair mention the fact that the KLA was set up by the Nazis to harass Serbia during German attempts to capture the Balkans during World War II. There was no mention either of the other activities of the KLA "freedom fighters." There was no mention that the KLA controlled, most if not all, of the drug and arms trade through the area. It could be said that the only reason Tony Blair and Bill Clinton could convince their supporters to accept this war was the fact that one of their friends in the press had branded the Serb leader Slobodan Milosevic as a fascist. It was truly amazing to see former sixties anti-war radicals led by a draft dodger screaming war cries at full shout while most politicians on the right were spouting anti-war rhetoric that could have been cribbed from the 60's. The hypocrisy of the 60s generation is nothing new and something I have documented in other parts of this work. I must point out that many of these self-same people were against the Gulf War (the liberation of an invaded sovereign nation). They were pro-Sandinista during the 80s and thus against the U.S. backed Contras (who were seeking to liberate their fellow countrymen from the iron rule of a dictator). A similar anomaly existed during the conflict in Afghanistan (the liberation of a land from an occupying power, the Soviets).

The real reason that Clinton and his allies were able to get away with this little excursion in the Balkans, is the same reason he was able to get away with the bombing of a medicine factory in Sudan (now the Clinton administration has admitted this was in error): playing on the ignorance of the general U.S. public. To most observers, it was clear that these actions were merely a method for Clinton to distract the citizens and others from his domestic pre and post impeachment problems related to the Monica Lewinski affair and his own personal failings.

Another aspect of foreign policy is foreign aid and the efficacy of the UN. To the internationalists who wish to spread the wealth anyone who appears to oppose massive aid is a labelled a neo-isolationist. Alas, this is a far too simplistic view of the argument. There is a perfectly reasonable reason to oppose massive money transfers from the American taxpayer to the government or people of another nation. If the U.S. government is able to give such large amounts of money out, this is a clear indication that the federal government has an excess of funds.

The only solution to such prodigal behaviour is limiting the amount of money the federal government receives in federal taxes and other levies. The money that is being given away by the President and Congress is not his to give away, but that of the people. If individuals wish to give money to one country or another they may do this through one of the many charities set up to aid almost every country on the planet. These organisations are efficient and reliable and unlike the federal government, are required to inform donors of exactly how much of their donation is getting to those in need. The largest amount of governmental foreign aide goes to the UN. Even under arch-internationalist Bill Clinton, the U.S. has defaulted on its payments to the organisation. It is unfortunate that the U.S. is not living up to agreements that it made, but as a nation we should not be in that position in the first place. The UN is notoriously anti-American in outlook and routinely sides with enemies of the U.S. It would be best if the U.S. were to pull out of the organisation and put the money it spends on

UN programs to better use by leaving it in the original owners' hands. That is to say the taxpayers' hands.

The UN and U.S. are in the habit of intervening in internal matters of other sovereign nations and in most cases making the situation worse and not better. The UN's failures in recent years are numerous: Somalia, Rwanda, the Balkans and the Middle East are just some of its more spectacular failures.

The same problem exists in the Middle East with Israel. While there are photo-ops at the White House with Israelis and Palestinians shaking hands, the reality on the ground in Israel is entirely different. How are the Palestinians expected to truly trust a President, with a party that so heavily relies on the support and funds of the Jewish community in the U.S.? The American President is unable to deliver on promises to pressure Israel into stopping Jewish settlements on the West Bank. Most of the settlers are either Americans or receive most of their financial support from American Jews.

The realities of American electoral politics are such that no American President can oversee any Mid-East negotiations without some level of prejudice or political pressure. It is impossible for an American politician to be neutral in these issues unless he or she comes from a state and a party that does not have or need the support of one or another of the ethnic group involved. This is the nature of the American experience as it is a nation of immigrants. Naturally there are people from almost every ethnic background in the world. It is preferable for those kinds of scenarios to be overseen by representatives from homogeneous countries such as Japan or Norway, who would be free from the pressures of ethnic lobbying groups.

There is another major deterrent to realistic views of the world by American politicians and the great American public. Both groups are very parochial in outlook. Whether it's our press or our education, Americans are an insular people, caring more about what is happening in there own State than what is happening across the world. Major problems in the world like the Indian-Pakistani conflict over the "line of control" in Kashmir do not even merit a mention. This despite the fact that both countries are new nuclear powers and have fought three bloody wars since their separation from the British Empire. Surely, the conflict and its aftermath merit greater mention in the media considering the global risks inherent in such conflicts.

The latest conflict, which cost each side thousands of lives and brought them to near all-out war, was mentioned in the American press only when the Pakistani Premier visited President Clinton to ask for U.S. help. One needs only to compare the BBC, ITN or Sky in the U.K. to the major networks in the U.S. to show the amount of news on the subject that American news media screened out from U.S. consumption. In the U.S., those truly interested in the world do not hear of war between Eritrea and Ethiopia, the slaughter of Christians in the Sudanese Civil War or ethnic strife in Indonesia, until well after the conflict has begun. Fortunately, the U.S. networks tend to use feeds from foreign networks, not even bothering to send their own people to these trouble spots. The coverage they do show is usually very good. Only when there are Americans involved, are events worth U.S. media notice and then they to go immediately to saturation coverage. The blinkered view of the world leads Americans to develop skewed views of how the world works. It also leads them to trust their leaders' ill-conceived forays into foreign arenas with little information about the actual situation at hand, until that is; Americans begin dying over there.

The media's excuse for not covering the world more fully is its lack of relevance to the Americans' daily lives. This ignorance and parochialism led Americans to elect two Southerners from small states: Bill Clinton and Jimmy Carter, with no Foreign Policy experience whatsoever. Disastrous results ensued. The networks claim that the public is not interested. Yet, time and again the American public has shown they do care. Good examples are the famines in Africa and earthquakes in Turkey and Greece. A major problem in the American networks is the extreme left-wing bias of the reporting staff. As with many other facets of American life, baby boomers are in charge there, too. It is curious to see that the major networks that filled the screen with the horrors of the Apartheid era in South Africa no longer care to report on the country as it falls into chaos. If one wishes to learn about today's South Africa and its problems with crime (the most violent country in the world by some estimates) and civil chaos, one must seek coverage from European networks.

It is possible that with the extension of high speed Internet access, Americans will take advantage of streaming video for foreign newscasts and educate themselves about events occurring beyond their borders. The major U.S. networks may be forced to tailor their news content to the interests of those watching or face losing more market share to the Internet. It is interesting to note that only one of the huge U.S. networks made a profit last year, NBC. This suggests that the networks are not delivering what viewers want, and thus not attracting a sufficient enough number of viewers to interest potential advertisers. That may be a good sign for the future.

Free trade is a major issue in the foreign policy arena. This is an area in which the U.S. has been recently acting like a spoiled child. While continuing to trade with China, a country that has stolen its own nuclear secrets and has an abysmal human rights record, we have chosen to retaliate and get into a trade war with Europe over genetically modified foods and banana subsidies. Rather than take the lead in this arena and pioneer free trade with all, we continue a policy of haphazard trade practices. There is still the possibility that these restructured policies could risk putting the world into a world-wide recession. Again, domestic politics play a great part in this policy. The Congress should be a leader in this arena and vote to accept imports from all non-hostile countries. Such a policy benefits the countries involved and the American consumer most of all. Protectionism as demonstrated by the

70's car industry in Detroit, does nothing to help the American people in the long run. Free trade forces American companies to be efficient and visionary, useful in the long run to both the industry sector involved, and the public as a whole through better, lower cost products.

8

Religion

This is a most contentious of issues and one that is theoretically a subject not to be discussed in a political context. Although it is hard at times to separate the two, religious beliefs need to be tempered when attempting to discuss politics, lest the discussion result in division on religious lines. There are those on both sides of the political spectrum who seem to strive to make religion a political issue. Of course our Puritan ancestors would disagree with this Jeffersonian belief in the separation of church and state.

The most recent iteration of this highly polarised and politicised debate occurred in Harrison County, Mississippi. Amazingly the incident occurred less than a week after Buford O'Neil, a so-called Identity Christian, shot up a Jewish nursery school, injuring tiny children, but thankfully, killing no one. The School Board in Harrison supported a local school that banned a male student from wearing a Star of David to school and then suspended him for refusing to follow the order. The Principal of the school held that the Jewish symbol could be construed as a "gang" symbol. The Chief of Security for the district praised the Principal, a Ms Parker, as being "proactive." Not only is Ms Parker an extremist and lacking in tact, she is also ignorant of precedent in such cases. A similar case occurred in 1997 in Texas regarding Catholic

Rosaries. A U.S. District Court Judge ruled in favour of the students. Rosaries and the Star of David are not normally associated with gang members and their symbols. [xxii]

In an ironic and interesting twist of fate, this matter has united Jerry Falwell, the ACLU and the Anti-Defamation League in the same corner. It is similar minded people who have purged any even slightly religious imagery from all public places. They are of course, opposed to children using state provided vouchers to go to Parochial schools despite the fact that in many cases this will be best for the child. In Michigan, school choice will help integrate the school system rather than segregate it. A poor black child attending a Catholic school will be more likely to attend school with students of other racial backgrounds than if he were to attend the public school system there, one of the most segregated in the country.

Of course, the other extreme does itself no favours either. Their pronouncements and actions range from foolish comical to near evil. The former being the case of Jerry Falwell claiming that one of the Teletubbies, Tinky Winky, is a gay icon because it (they are meant to be sexless) carries a red pocket book-like bag, is coloured purple (a colour not normally associated with homosexuality, pink or rainbows being the colouring of choice) and has a triangle on his head. He claims that Tinky Winky is meant to familiarise small children with homosexuals and lead them to accept them. Bear in mind that this program is aimed at the under fives and was developed and popularised in the U.K. Mr. Falwell has not latched onto the more curious fact that the program appears to be a 30 minute long acid trip. It seems to have been written while under the influence of hallucinogens. In fact the program has a cult following among drug using college students on both sides of the Atlantic.

In an attempt to make themselves look idiotic and hypocritical (one can only assume) a group of organisations led by Paul Weyrich, President of Free Congress, that includes the Christian Coalition, the

Traditional Values Association and American Family Association, are attempting to prevent American military personnel from practising Wicca. They claim that the Army should not be a haven for "Satanists" and that an Army that "sponsors satanic rituals is unworthy of representing the U.S.A." It is obvious to anyone with even a rudimentary knowledge of non-Judeo-Christian religion that Wiccans are no such thing. They are in fact a pre-Christian form of nature worship, similar to that practised by Druids and American Indians. This type of campaign is not original. The Catholic Church demonised Wiccans in Europe to discredit pagan and female centred religions. Mr. Weyrich seems intent to stir up anti-witch type hysteria that was prevalent in the middle ages and early America. Does he really think modern day Wiccans sacrifice small children? It is clear that Mr. Weyrich has no idea what a Satanist is and would not be able to identify one if he met one. [xxiii]

Examples such as these demonstrate that many on the religious right have as little respect for the Constitution as those on the socialist left. It is also these people who tout the myth that the U.S. was founded as a Christian country. In fact many of the founding fathers were adamantly against any sort of reference to any deity or facet of religion other than God in the document. At the constitutional convention, a prayer was proposed and rejected, Benjamin Franklin having noted that "only 3 or 4 supported it." Alexander Hamilton is on record as having suggested that there was no need for the help of a "foreign power." At the time there was a clear attempt to end the religious persecution that non "Congregationalists" had suffered in the Americas during its history, up to that time. It is widely known that the Puritans were intolerant to the point of exiling a "heretic" on sentence of death upon return. A "heretic" was anyone who was not a Puritan. (Hence the term Puritanical). Most of the original 13 states denied the vote to men who were Jews, Deists, Catholics and unbelievers. Five of the states forced their citizens, regardless of their own beliefs to tithe to local churches by law, and of course there were several states that were almost exclusively one religion, such as Rhode Island. [xxiv]We know that Jefferson was a Deist [xxv]and not a Christian. He made it clear in his writings that he was very anti-establishment church.

Surely every American has the right to worship in any way he or she chooses as long as it does not directly affect others? What about the right to free association? It seems many of the modern Protestant organisations believe in these rights, but only for those with Judaeo-Christian beliefs. They have gotten over their anti-Catholic and anti-Semitic feelings (at least publicly) but retain a hatred for anything they see as Pagan.

Scientologists, believers in the teachings of L Ron Hubbard from his book *Dianetics*, often come under fire in the mainstream media. In recent years high profile Hollywood celebrities, such as John Travolta, have gone some way in deflecting media scrutiny.

The more worrying of these mainstream fundamentalists are the Westboro Baptist Church and its <u>www.godshatesfags.com</u> website[xxvi] and campaigning group. The organisation led by Pastor Phelps prides itself on public displays of anti-homosexual protest, culminating in their protest at the funeral of the openly gay college student, Matthew Shepard. In case there is some mistake about their opinion of the young man, his picture has been placed in moving flames with the following message below it: "If this doesn't work, hear Matthew's message from hell!" Most Christians are appalled by this behaviour, but the organisation continues to receive press and financial support. The site has been visited almost one million times. Other politically active ministers whose pronouncements can be as extreme as Mr. Phelps' are the Rev. Al Sharpton and the Rev. Jesse Jackson. Both of these men pride themselves on using every tragedy with the slightest trumped-up racial facet to further their own political aims.

Another Christian group occasionally under the lime-light for its unusual beliefs, are the Boston based Christian Scientists. These Christians, who believe in the power of faith healing over modern medicine, tend to only come under fire when a child dies due to alleged neglect via lack of modern medical care.

Christians are not alone in their extremism. Louis Farrakan and his Nation of Islam are routinely allowed to speak their anti-Semitic and anti-white rhetoric. Much of the content on the Nation of Islam web-site does not differ much from that contained on the sites of "Identity" or "Seedline Christians." Both groups share the belief that Jews are directly descended from Satan via Cain, (anyone with an interest in vampire lore, might be surprised by this, as it is thought that it was vampires, otherwise known as Cainites, that were the ones descended from Cain). The groups differ only on whom they regard as the Jews' slaves (the latter group refers to "Mudpeople" or non-whites while the former group refers to white people). Although, these men have a right to free speech, it is unfortunate for real Muslims living in the U.S. that this type of slander is seen as typical of their faith. When these activities are added to the anti-American terrorism of some Islamic extremists it is no wonder Muslims and their faith are very poorly understood amongst the wider U.S. public.

Extremism in Judaism was almost unknown publicly until the murder of Israeli Prime Minister Izak Rabin a few years ago. Because of this tragic event, media attention was focused on the extremism of radical Jewish settlers and the fact that much of their financial sup-port comes from the U.S. As with other such groups, like the Irish Republican Army, the internet is heavily used to gather U.S. based financial support.

Abortion is the other issue that causes the most heat in the U.S. polit-ical arena. It would seem to any observer that the entire nation is polarised between people who believe that a child can be aborted up to and including the time it is about to be born, while the other side wishes to ban all abortion for whatever reason, preferably by changing the con-stitution. The truth, of course, is that most people fall somewhere in the middle, believing that abortion is generally a bad thing, not a smart thing to use as a contraceptive and preferably not done. It is only the most obstinate who believe that abortion is wrong in the case of rape, incest or threat to the life of the mother.

This debate was at its most ludicrous when the Senate and House of Representatives debated the banning of late-term abortions. The pro-side decried a ban as "the thin edge of the wedge," while their opponents promised that this was just the first step in the outright banning of abortion in totality. Most sensible people were amazed that anyone could possibly defend the practice of late term abortions. However there was enough heat generated by the abortion on demand crowd that the bill failed in the Senate. The truth turns out to be that this practice rarely if ever occurs. The whole imbroglio was manufactured by both sides. Despite what both sides believe, it is possible to be in favour of abortion, against federal funding of the practice and anti-using abortion as a form of contraception. Most people after all are pretty middle of the road on such difficult issues involving the intersection of life and moral tenets.

It is difficult for anyone who believes in freedom to attempt to dictate to a woman what she should do with her own body. Of course, it is equally unreasonable for that woman to expect the taxpayer to pay for an abortion. It is entirely reasonable for those who pay the bill, to have a say in how the money is spent and why. Abortion should not now or ever be an issue in which the State has any right to meddle. The State neither belongs in the bedroom, the womb or the hospital, nor should the State be responsible for righting any individual mistakes made in these arenas.

The media are to blame as much as the churches in these incendiary discussions. The media seem to revel in religious extremism, reporting with gusto the mass suicides of the Jim Jones' group, the Order of the Solar Temple, the Branch Davidians and Heaven's Gate. [xxvii]As we near the end of the millennium, there will be more of these groups vying for attention and the oxygen of mass publicity. Some of these groups will attempt to get this attention and push the world towards the Christian end of the world scenario (Armageddon) by perpetrating extreme acts of violence.

The problem with religion in America is that much of its more reasonable iterations are hidden from view. The public sees the more ridiculous versions in religion in the form of tele-evangelists and fundamentalists on the Internet. Many of these Protestants seek to turn modern American evangelical Christianity into a return to the Christianity of the dark ages, based on superstition, miracles, absolute unquestioning loyalty and adherence to the charismatic minister. That belief is meant to be absolute, unthinking, radically evangelical and chauvinistic. Rather than bolster their belief with careful study and scholarship, communicants are encouraged to take whatever interpretation they are handed as the only true interpretation. It is this sort of belief that allows it to be acceptable for a evangelical Christian to publicly accost a man wearing a Catholic cross and carrying a rosary, yelling at him that he will be going "to hell with Hitler, Stalin, the Pope and Madonna," as occurred recently to a Roman Catholic acquaintance of mine.

Of most interest to those concerned with freedom, are the groups who seek to turn the U.S. into a theocracy. Some are extremist groups listed above. Others are in the near mainstream, such as the Christian Coalition. These people are as Statist as their socialist opposites on the other side of the political aisle. They seek through the use of the State to dictate how Americans may live, love and lead their lives. The Christian Statists are as much a threat to freedom in the U.S. as any "big-government loving" socialists. It is curious that both groups claim to be seeking anti-liberty government policies for the same reason: in order to protect society from itself. Both groups liberally use the constitution and the founding fathers to justify their actions, with little care for accuracy. The founding fathers of the United States did not envision a country completely secular and purged of all hints of religion nor did they envision a Christian country with a State run along Protestant Christian lines.

Religion and belief can be a positive and helpful aspect of an individual's life. It is however counter-productive and a direct threat to freedom when it takes on its fundamentalist form. Secularism has its fundamentalist form as well, and is equally dangerous and extreme. Secularism and religion that seek to usurp an individual's right to freedom of speech and expression, is as much an anathema to the principals of freedom and that of the U.S. as the prospect of the U.S. becoming a Protestant theocracy.

Religion is a matter between an individual and his or her beliefs and not something in which the State should be involved except to protect the free expression and practice there-of.

9

Law & Order

One of the other great issues in the U.S. today is law and order. More accurately, it is the debate over how to keep order so that life and commerce can go on without restricting the rights of ordinary citizens to conduct their lives as they please. One of the few jobs of the State, in classical liberal theory, is the protection of property and commerce. The State is improving its efforts to rectify the increases in crimes against property and commerce that were seen in the 70's and 80's. It is clear that part of the reason for the decrease in crime is that "baby boomer" males have surpassed the age at which they are most likely to commit crime (ages: 15–24). Programs such as California's "three strikes and you're out" have helped take criminals off the streets, political crimes and "victimless" crimes included. A study conducted in 1998 concluded that violent crime dropped 26.9% and murders were down by 40% since the law was introduced in 1994. [xxviii]

We do continue to allow inmates to sue their jailers for lack of provisions and trivial comfort issues. Thankfully, both major parties have read the disgust of their constituents and are seeking ways of making the criminal justice system more sensitive to the needs of the victim rather than focusing solely on the criminal as a poor wayward person.

For libertarians, this subject includes their most contentious issue, capital punishment. Pure libertarians do not believe that the State should commit murder in the name of its citizens, i.e. exercise a death penalty. While this is an admirable argument, it runs into difficulties at the extreme such as a serial killer like Charles Manson or Ted Bundy. What possible justification can there be for the State spending millions of taxpayer dollars to keep these individuals alive and living in relative comfort at taxpayers' expense.

Add to this the problem of social workers who imagine that they see only the best in people and you have an explosive mixture that has seen something close to the return of establishment lynch mobs in some communities. As mentioned earlier, there is a solution to the problem of criminals who are released early and who err again. Those who support the release of the individual should be held criminally and financially liable for any actions perpetrated by the freed former inmate. If the individual kills again, the social worker that supported his or her release should be charged with accessory manslaughter or a similar offence. As it stands now, there is no sanction for those individuals who support the release of a violent criminal. Fortunately, after the public outcry following a few high profile cases, judges and parole boards seem to be less willing to take chances on the more serious criminals.

What is the solution to mass murderers? There are many that feel execution is the wrong solution to the problem. There would be no debate if a life sentence meant life. It does rarely in modern times. The other problem with keeping these individuals alive is the threat of escape. As has been proven many times, no jail is totally secure. The one positive outcome of execution is that the criminal will never be able to kill again. There are those who argue that executions do not deter others from committing similar crimes, and they point out that there is possibility of the innocent being executed unjustly. It does however prevent recidivism.

It could be argued that executions should be made public and broadcast to all who cared to watch. This spectacle, while crude, would serve as a reminder to the young of what can happen if he or she chooses a life of violent crime. This is the ultimate "scared straight" program. While the death penalty should not be the penalty for all murder, it should be a viable option for those who commit multiple murders. Is it right that taxpayers should pay the $40,000 a year to support these people who should never be released? Perhaps we should go back to the system of a remote island penal colony where the worst criminals govern themselves, and survive or not.

A similarly troubling group of criminals are paedophiles and child murderers. As part of their reintegration into society many are put in care homes in residential districts. New laws now force local governments to disclose the presence of a paedophile in the town in which he lives. For the more serious cases, there have been incidents where citizens have driven the person out of their community. This is a logical reaction by parents who rightly feel these child-predators are threats to their families. In these cases, the rights of the many should outweigh those of the one. Is it right that an entire neighbourhood or town must now keep their children inside at all times? Is it right that this individual ruins the framework of a town because of his so-called right to live in society? The situation is caused in part by the much-debated theory that such criminals can be cured or deterred by prison time. It seems clear that the only deterrent is the prison itself.

There continue to be major problems with the scope of the law enforcement in the country. Police continue to harass motorists on the highway, while seemingly ignoring other types of crime. There are those in government who still believe that constitutional rights to free speech and to bear arms need to be curtailed. Neither party seeks to either repeal laws against cannabis or end the ludicrous drinking age limit of 21 years. Then there is the case of censorship, one that is becoming ever more of a problem with advent of the Internet.

The so-called "War on Drugs," started by a Republican President has been continued by a Democratic one. What makes this situation all the more bizarre are that many of those who helped elect Bill Clinton were at the forefront of drug use in the 1960's. There is ample evidence that both the President and the Vice President indulged in marijuana smoking as teenagers and beyond, yet they continue to pursue the losing battle that is the "war on drugs." While the U.S. government pours money into Latin American countries and their corrupt police forces, it does little or nothing to stem the tide of customers in their own country. Trafficking has become so profitable that most if not all of the terrorist groups in South America now traffic in drugs for income to buy weapons and ammunition. In some cases, these organisations are earning hundreds of millions of dollars a year via this trade. Keeping these drugs illegal hands the traffickers vast sums of money. This so-called war is a complete defeat. The trade is now corrupting the elected governments of South American countries. The "War on Drugs" has not done very much to reduce the availability or increase the price of drugs. It is still possible anywhere in America to acquire your drug of choice with little or no effort or danger of detection.

There have been some moves in the direction of marijuana legalisation but this bizarre obfuscation is comical and counter-productive. In many states, it is now possible to carry pot if the amount is small enough to be for "personal use." Thus in these states it has become the case of: "it is okay to break the law as long as you don't do it in a big way!" Surely this is a ludicrous way to enforce a law. Any encouragement to violate laws sets bad precedent. Would it not be better to legalise the substance, enact strict "pot driving" laws, and allow it to be a commercial product? Another amusing recent development is the so-called "medical marijuana" laws. Instead of legalising it for all, many states are now considering or have passed laws that allow those with a medical reason to acquire the drug. Naturally, the number of people with certified conditions is likely to rise exponentially, as seen in

California recently. A significant anomaly is that federal law still prohibits cannabis use and its prescription by medical doctors.

The most logical solution to this problem is the legalisation of the drug. Tobacco or pharmaceutical companies can market it and then the states can tax it as they do tobacco. States are losing hundreds of thousands of tax dollars each year that they could be getting from cannabis sales. After we legalise marijuana, then the country might be able to have an intelligent discussion about the viability of the legalisation of other drugs.

In some arenas, the above suggestion immediately evokes the example of Amsterdam and the chaos lax drug laws have caused there. Those who use this example fail to mention that Holland, through it's socialist social policy finds itself forced to support those who become addicted to hard drugs (heroin, cocaine, amphetamines and crack). As a result, Amsterdam has attracted addicts from all over Europe; to have their habit supported by the taxpayers of Holland, through free heroin distribution. The solution to this problem is that the federal government and the states should make it clear, that anyone who becomes an addict will be on his own. If he or she commits a crime to support that habit, then the addiction will not be taken into account during sentencing. It must be made clear to the individual that he or she makes a choice in injecting, swallowing, smoking or snorting the substance consumed. It is no one's fault but their own, that they in turn became an addict and turned to crime to support that habit. Ditto with resulting health problems like malnutrition.

As stated earlier, sensible laws on drinking would alleviate many of the problems involving that other drug of choice, alcohol. We must lower the drinking age to 18 and maybe even lower. Then the country must make an effort to stop treating drinking as a sin and treat as a normal part of human existence. If we no longer turn young adults into criminals for having a drink, they will be less likely to break other laws. It is clear that once an individual has taken the step to break one law it is much easier to break another. This is an argument against foolishly low rural highway speed limits as well. It is logical that an individual who spends time with underage drinkers who are violating the law, is more likely to come into contact with other law breakers, even if it's simply so that they may acquire the drink. Would it not be more sensible to allow these individuals to be a part of normal society and go to bars where they will be in a controlled and structured environment? Surely it is nonsensical to tell young adults and children that alcohol is evil yet when they turn 21 it is suddenly acceptable. Why not teach children gradually the acceptable use of alcohol? Isn't that the procedure we use in trying to teach children to drive a car?

Closely related to the debate over alcohol is the debate over the Constitutional right to bear arms. There are those who say that this ancient, historical right of all Americans is outdated. Those who are on that bandwagon believe the entire Constitution to be outdated or in their parlance "dead," and thus irrelevant. With every new case of the criminally insane shooting multiple victims, the anti-gun crowd cries louder. With the advent of school killings, the hue and cry now has the added to the fervour of gun control as being "for the children." Never mind the fact that in all these cases those who committed the crimes violated countless laws well before the shooting occurred. Still the incidents are a great springboard for demands for more gun control. Until now, the Supreme Court has taken the 2nd Amendment literally. How long can the Court resist pressure from the anti-gun lobby?

All the rights enshrined in the Constitution are of equal value in my opinion. In calling for the 2nd Amendment to be overturned and slandering those who support it, these people invoke the 1st Amendment. Surely it is dangerous to tamper with any part of the original Bill of Rights. Do we really want to take guns away from law-abiding citizens? If we do take guns from average citizens, only criminals and the police will have the guns? Our ancestors clearly saw that situation as a clear danger to free citizens. The whole purpose of the 2nd Amendment is to ensure that the people may overthrow a tyrannical government. It should be legal for any U.S. citizen to own any weapon he or she cares to own. If he uses it in an illegal fashion then the law should be invoked and the person should be held accountable for his actions. Until such time as he commits a crime, he is innocent and should be able to own any weapon he chooses. The government has no right to prevent a law-abiding citizen from having these items. It is surely clear that this is the purpose of the 2nd Amendment. In fact, the history of the time proves out the intent of the framers of the Constitution. It is a basic part of the rights of all Americans to bear arms. Those of us who believe in the Constitution must resist the hate speech being peddled by opponents of this most basic of American freedoms. Gun owners and members of the NRA are not criminals or extremists but citizens exercising their rights under the Constitution. Please note that no responsible citizens condone or seek to hide irresponsible or criminal behaviour whether perpetrated with a gun or an axe. An axe figures prominently as the murder weapon in a case in Massachusetts well over a hundred years ago. In today's climate of knee-jerk legislation, all axes of whatever size used would subsequently have been banned from individual possession and use.

The latest area of difficulty for the law and its enforcement is the Internet and modern communications. The law and lawyers are behind the times when it comes to technical issues and have a hard time keeping up with the new technology. Much of the law in this area is based on older technology and does not reflect the change that is occurring. A major problem for both Internet Service Providers and the State is Internet site content. Under whose jurisdiction does it lie? Is content the responsibility of the ISP or that of the individual? May an ISP censor the information its users display and to which they have access? Although there has been debate over the latter problem, the answer is clearly, yes. A private company may restrict use of its service as it sees fit. If the customer does not like it, he may complain of course, but may also seek another service provider. There have been court cases covering this issue, but most have been frivolous. Some court decisions have resulted from lack of understanding of the Internet's characteristics on the part of judge and jury. As an example, the parents in one case sued their ISP for damages because several fellow students had rated their daughters on their looks on their web page. In the industry there is room for ISP's who allow access to everything and anything and those who cater for prudes. As long as the company clearly posts its policy towards content, they should not be liable for the content on their sites or the sites that can be accessed through their server.

The Internet most often comes under attack in discussions relating to pornography. There are those who hold that the Internet is mostly porn and nothing else. Sadly, these people are missing out on good entertainment, conversation and news, as well as a valuable additional research tool.

School and town libraries have been under fire for years from the citizens who feel it is their responsibility to censor the reading of other citizens. With the Internet, this fervour to control has taken on a new twist.

Of course, some of the problem is centred on the continuing controversial definition of pornography. It seems society's definition of what is pornography, is not clear. What is clear is that some citizens, many located in the south, see the classics as pornographic. Fine for them and for their children, as they are responsible for their children. However, other parents may have a different definition of what material is acceptable for their children. The first group should not be given control over the second group. If the restricting parents feel so strongly about what they feel is objectionable then they may remove their children from school and either home-school (which many are doing) or send them to parochial school (vouchers and tax relief should help offer choices to these parents). Included with so-called pornographic books (i.e. the classics) is so-called satanic literature and games. A group of parents in

Minneapolis, Minnesota have successfully forced a local school to ban JK Rowling's highly popular Harry Potter series of books, on grounds they are "evil." Harry the main character in the books is a wizard. [xxix] If one were to ban all works that contain a supernatural element, we would lose most of the great works. Books such as Macbeth, the works of Edgar Allan Poe, much of Sir Arthur Conan Doyle, the Bible and the Koran (as well as most other major religious texts) would have to fall under such a ban.

10

Different year, same old same old.

The convention season is officially not long past and we have seen some bizarre behaviour from both major parties. The Reform Party has been acting in an odd manner but then we never knew what they were reforming.

The Reformers are split over who is entitled to receive the 12 million dollars in US federal matching funds that they are set to receive. At this point, the two camps, Perot and Buchanan are holding separate conventions and suing each other over who gets the spoils. What do American taxpayers think of all this squabbling of who is going to get taxpayer to run a hopeless campaign that will barely make a dent in the final votes? Surely if people wish to spend their time in a Quixotic pursuit, they should be expected to pay for it themselves. It is hard to criticize however as GWB, who raised a record amount of money for his campaign, has decided to take matching funds for his general election run. In trade for spending limits, GWB's campaign will receive many millions of dollars in taxpayer money to support the candidate's run to the White House.

The Republicans and Democrats are in the midst of exchanging clothes with one or other. Using the language and spin of each other's party to try to attract the mythical center of American politics. What is so amusing is that both parties must talk to their "base" at the convention, by definition further from the center than the average American, all the while appearing to publicly be moving to the center. This year, it looks as if the Republicans, a run by George W Bush, have managed this trick better that Gore and Co. GWB continued his attempt to paint the Republicans as caring with his "compassionate conservatism." Why anyone would put up with this banner is confusing. By definition the term implies that conservatives are normally not compassionate. How very insulting! In a bizarre twist a "conservative" was selected as vice-president the former Defense Secretary Dick Cheney. However somehow it got out that his daughter is a lesbian. The only real "controversy" was the fact that a pro-wrestler was going to call the session to order one day at the Convention. One of the most humorless groupings in the party, protested against this as they were not fans of professional wrestling. The wrestler went ahead. The forces who wish to have the Republican, a party for those under 60 triumphed.

Republicans of all ilks, in their desperation regain the White House, have taken the bait and swallowed. As are result, the RNC in Philadelphia looked more like a NSync or Britney Spears concert than a political convention. Unlike its UK yearly counterpart, the Conservative Party Conference, there was no organized fringe scene run by dissident Republicans, and not much discussion at all. I understand that if one was not part of a state delegation (delegate or alternate) there was little if anything to do. I suppose one could always go and watch the police beat up protestors, or attend one of the two alternative conventions going on, if one dared. The threatened union strike in Philly, a heavily Democrat and old left town, never materialized. This was no doubt due to the fact that all the good socialist union workers were too busy working on overtime pay to be able to strike.

In LA, home of the majority of Friends of Bill, Al Gore and the Democrats are having a much harder time with their own balancing act. Gore is attempting to take credit for all the "good" things that the

Clinton administration did for the country while at the same time distancing himself from his boss Bill. His selection of Joseph Lieberman, Senator from Connecticut, has gotten him into trouble as well. Lieberman was brought onto the ticket to add moral character, so that Gore can distance himself from the problems of the Clinton administration. The announcement of his selection, became almost a prayer meeting that would have made Jerry Falwell pleased. Lieberman claims to be a man of faith, however his voting record in the Senate puts him fore-square with his democratic colleagues.

The Senator has another problem. He is one of the most vocal critics of the entertainment industry. In the Republican Party, this would not be a problem. However some of the largest donors to the Democrat Party make their money in the industry he so vociferously criticizes. One must also remember that Al Gore's wife was a founding member of the arch-censorious group, responsible for parental warning stickers on music, the Parent Music Resource Center. It is clear that the politicos believe that young adults have no memory of the PMRC and its actions. In my experience, young adults *do* remember the people responsible for their being blocked from the music they favoured when they were young. One can only imagine what censorious schemes Tipper and Joe are going to dream up, if Gore ticket is elected in November.

Mr. Lieberman, a man of so-called high moral values is Jewish was Clinton's biggest critic in the Senate and fundamentally disagrees with Gore on many issues. Add to this, the Black anti-Semitism (head of the Dallas NAACP and Rep Maxine Waters being the most vociferous) that is emanating from under the carpet and Gore is losing control. To makes matter worse Clinton, is unwilling or unable to pass the baton. Various left of left groups planned riots outside the convention center, attempting to do their best to relive the glories of the 67 Democratic Convention.

It is not hard to imagine that the Conventions could turn out this way. The nominee is pre-determined by Primary-Caucus season. The candidate is selected and the Vice-Presidential choice is announced before the convention even begins. There is really no point to the affair besides an excuse for the major political parties to get the taxpayer of which ever city loses (rather wins) the selection process to host the affair. In fact, the convention has become some sort of perk for the activist party faithful. No wonder news coverage and viewer interest has dropped with each election cycle.

Even those activists do not always fare well.

The Republicans managed to select a city totally unsuited for the convention. Many delegates were housed in hotels in another state, New Jersey. These had to be bused in every morning through rush hour traffic across one of the most congested bridges in the world to get to the convention hall.

While the Reform Party, Pat Buchanan and their antics get copious amounts of coverage in the press, and Ralph "Unsafe at any Speed" Nader receives a decent amount of coverage of his and the Green Parties Marxism light agenda, the Libertarian Party is virtually ignored. Their candidate for President, Harry Browne, has caught up in some polls to both Nader and Buchanan, despite total apathy from the press. It is the Libertarian's own fault, truth be told. Their convention was much too sedate. There was no rioting, fighting, huge great row or protest. If the party's ideas were really spread in the US, there would be a great deal of controversy in the media. After all we are talking about a party which calls for the abolition of income tax and the IRS. It is possible the party may be in a position to get more attention if Carla Howell, Edward Kennedy's only opponent for Senate in Massachusetts, does well against the veteran senator. The party recently launched a series of hard hitting cable television ads against big government.

To be frank, nothing has changed in 2000. The major parties still, plod along avoiding a single thought or idea. The media, mostly left of center in outlook, goes along with being spoon fed their new content for the convention. The major networks use their falling Convention audience figures to justify even less coverage each time, allowing the all-news and on-line networks to take up the slack and provide the proper coverage of these "events".

Both the Republicans and the Democrats continue to patronize and ignore anyone under 35, while spending all their time talking about "young people." At least at the Republican National Convention, Young Republicans were absorbed into their state's delegations and but for a few parties the YRs did not really exist at the Convention. The state will be even bigger after a Bush or Gore administration, it is no longer a case of *if* but how much the increase will be in 2004. Neither party talks about giving the American back his rights as a citizen. The Constitution barely merits a mention in any speech heard on the floor. It is not about ideas, it is about winning, winning at all costs. The parties may win or lose but in the end the only loser in the American citizen. Only at the Libertarian Convention is the Constitution present as the honored guest next to the flag in importance, all candidates reflecting on the virtues of both.

Statism sucks but no one in power in the two major parties believes it. We can be certain of one thing, until things change, we will lose more and more of our rights and the federal and state government will continue getting larger and larger. Depressing isn't it? Will it take a revolution to change things? Wait till the next recession.

With the government spending increases, especially in states, like Maine, the next recession will be disastrous, deep and prolonged. Will the government squandering of the fruits of increased productivity and repression of citizen rights and responsibilities produce citizen backlash. That could happen.

Epilogue

This treatise was born out of the frustration with situations I have witnessed or have been a party to both in the U.K. and in the U.S. This includes personal experiences with heavy handed intervention both by liberal arts college administrators and by government bureaucracy.

I have been collecting ideas and forming opinions over the years. Many of these thoughts were developed in political discussions and editorials since my graduation from university. I first examined these ideas in a trilogy about a decaying European Union some thirty years into the new century.

A few examples: It is May 1987. A professor with whom a student disagreed politically (she has a bumper sticker on her office door proclaiming: "Africa says thank you Fidel Castro"), accused the student of cheating on his final exam. Her accusation tool took the form of an announcement during the exam and was clearly aimed to publicly humiliate the student. After several witnesses supported his innocence and other professors vouched for his character, the first professor recanted the charge and but failed the student anyway. There was a little known rule that allowed professors to fail students without appeal for any reason. The student was denied a fair hearing in front of an academic board, thus tarnishing his reputation academically and publicly.

In February of 1988, a group of Colby Professors pressured the College administrators to ban the U.S. Central Intelligence Agency from interviewing job-seeking students on campus saying the action was because of their "unethical" and "morally repugnant" behaviour. Most students were against this move and protested. Some of those involved managed to get the national press including the television media to come to this remote campus to report on the controversy. After several members of the student opposition were featured on television and in print, the professors backed down. They certainly were getting bad publicity. However, many of these professors pursued personal vendettas against their opposition both in the student body and fellow professors. One strong opponent of the anti-CIA measure was driven out of his tenured position very quickly thereafter.

The United Kingdom has of course many of the same reasonable laws found in North America and Europe to assure due process for citizens: now called human rights. A recent experience so contravened those principles the even the uninitiated could have seen that my rights were violated. Due process and normal courtesy were replaced by anti-American ethnicism, class warfare angst and arrogance on the part of an official. It was clear to me that the officer knew he could violate my rights and regulations governing the immigration service and would automatically get away with it. The outcome was clear when the officer threatened to have me arrested immediately, a power which I later learned he did not have at his disposal. He continued to interrogate me for most of 6 hours using many classic psychological techniques you may have seen in the movies: a type of bait and switch questioning, fiddling with papers to distract me and insults too egregious to mention. The officer also forbade other station officers from allowing my mother to accompany me into the station waiting room, contrary to the treatment afforded all other individuals being questioned there at that time.

The U.K. Immigration law requires that the person questioned review the officer's report of the session and sign indicating that the statements represented were his. Just as well that the officer skipped that requirement. He had completely falsified my statements so as to produce a near textbook "scenario" to keep me out of the U.K. He surely continues to treat immigrants in a way never contemplated by U.K. law and his superiors have thus far refused to acknowledge a loose cannon in their ranks.

Conclusions

Throughout this work, I have tried to critique some of the problems existing in politics and government in the late 90's. I have also tried to offer some solutions to the problems I have highlighted. I admit that, in many of parts of this treatise, I have only offered more questions. If you find this a little thought provoking, then I have accomplished my purpose. If you are also clarifying your own political philosophy in light of what you have read here, and you plan to use your new power when you vote, I applaud you!

The Republican Party states its aims to lower taxes and reduce governmental involvement, while doing little or nothing about either. The Democrats, now espouse policies designed to take freedom away from the individual and hand it back to their once hated enemy: the state. To make matters worse, these born-again Statists now conspire to send the American and British military into every civil war on the planet. What ever happened to "make peace, not war?" Wasn't that the mantra of the 60's generation?

As we begin the New Year and celebrate the new millennium (2000 or 2001, take your pick) we need to re-evaluate how we wish to be governed and how free we wish to be in the future. We, as a nation, and as a culture, need to disengage ourselves from the block interests that plague both the U.S. and the U.K. We need to find philosophical solutions before making plans to solve problems. Without philosophical underpinning the solutions are too often seen as money, money and more money, but the problems then just get worse.

As the baby boomers grow older and move aside, (Is this wishful thinking?) the next generation will be able to put its stamp on the leadership of this country. We will be able to pare back the state to the low profile intended in the Constitution. We will take inspiration from the founding fathers. We must take up their call and turn this country into the "classical liberal" paradise that the founding fathers intended it should be, and as a working example to other nations. Then, we will be able to pursue real freedom, that is freedom with responsibility for all citizens.

With the precedent of the internet, we will be able to pare back the oppressive laws that are passed everyday by the bloated bureaucracy that are the U.S. and U.K. governments and others. We must re-examine the issue of states' rights and the power of the central government. We should look again to the Federalist Papers and seek their guidance on these issues. Through a major change in the taxation system we can change government into the force that it was meant to be, instead of a hydra sucking every last ounce of freedom from its citizens. The state is very similar to an addict. It is a collective addict, addicted to increasing money and power. This American generation needs to force the U.S. Government into a new version of the "Betty Ford Clinic," to dry out cold turkey. Starve the state of money, and it will shrink, reluctantly, but it will shrink, like a dying taxation hydra.

We need to think again of ourselves as Americans, not as each a member of a sectionalised minority group culled from the majority and set aside. We must end the destructive tendency of separating people from the majority and then pitting them against each other. No more special favours for any group. We need to work to make it so that every individual citizen can have as much freedom as he can use responsibly. Reduce the power of the state, hand power over to the citizen, stopping short of anarchy but only just. Criminals, who abuse these freedoms, must be dealt with in a swift and forceful manner that discourages others from the same course of action.

If we do not change the way the U.S. is governed, we face the realistic prospect of revolution, civil war or secession. We, in the U.S. must take a good look at the former Soviet Union, Yugoslavia and tensions for separation in the European Union. It is impossible to keep people together who do not want to be together except by force. Forcing people out of the mainstream results in more incidents of domestic terrorism.

As individuals, we need to re-assert our personal responsibility over our lives and stop allowing others to do it for us. We need to take responsibility for our actions and not expect others to clean up our messes. We need to take back our rights from the state by voting en masse for politicians who are willing to assert and stand up for the absolute freedom of the individual. We must elect politicians who will target the laws they will abolish, rather than laws that they wish to pass. If they fail in this duty we should remove them at the next election and choose someone else for the job. We, as a nation of individual citizens, must take advantage of that right given to all of us by the Constitution and vote in every election.

As parents, we need to take back parenting and education from the State and the unions. We need to take care of our children and make sure we plan to be responsible for their education and for their well being before they are born. As mothers and fathers, we need to see the job through that we signed up for when we first produced the child; raising it to the best of our ability till the child reaches adulthood. We need to push to abolish the failure that is the public school system and either take our children out of bad schools and send them to private schools or teach them at home. We must, as parents and alumni of universities all over country, threaten to stop donating money unless the schools treat their students as individuals and not the automatons in Fritz Leiber's "Metropolis." Free speech for all must make a comeback on college campuses.

As we enter our third century as a nation we need to re-evaluate what we wish to be as a nation. We need to grow up and join the family of adult nations. We need to stop acting as though America is a teenager patronised on issues of sex, drugs and personal freedom. The nation needs to grow up and realise that it no longer needs to prove itself "mature." In short, we as a nation need to start treating Americans as adults capable of knowing what is best for themselves and their children. The Declaration of Independence clearly states that we as human beings have the inalienable right to "Life, Liberty, and the PURSUIT of Happiness." It does not, and neither should the government, attempt to guarantee happiness.

It is time to grow up, leave home and act like responsible adults!

About the Author

Andrew Ian Dodge is a 32 year-old Harpswell based novelist/writer and sole proprietor of Lupus & Co, a web-based publishing house. His writing career as Marty Dodge began as a rock reviewer for several local rock magazines on the East Coast of the US. This followed a 4 year tenure, while at Colby College, as WMHB's Metal Director/Metal DJ. He writes reviews for hard rock electronic-magazine, SFK. Marty Dodge is a game expert for Internet based Macintosh magazine: MacUnlimited.com and has written a future gaming column for the UK-based print magazine, MacFormat. He has written 4 novels and book of short stories.

Politically, Andrew Ian Dodge has held various offices in the Young Conservatives (UK) inc. at the local level (Secretary), area (Vice Chairman) and national executive (Social Secretary). He is currently Chairman, and a former treasurer, of the Maine Young Republicans. In addition he has experience in political campaigning in both the US and the UK at all levels. He is widely traveled and speaks Spanish fluently as well as a smattering of French.

A self described Deist and Radical Liberal (modern libertarian) of the late 1800s, his mode of dress is eccentric and mannerisms harken back to gentlemen of the 19th century. His politics are for very limited government, a flat tax, laissez faire economics and a return to the ideals of the Constitution, together with its inspiration, the Age of Reason. To wit his calling card reads simply: Cynic, Cyberpunk and Raconteur.

Footnotes

[i] John McCaslin, *Inside the Beltway* , Washington Times Online (5th July 1999)World News Communications Washington, D.C. www.washtimes.com/politics/politics.html.

[ii] David Boaz, *Libertarianism: A Primer* ([New York] Free Press 1998.)

[iii] Scott Parks, *NM Governor says Drug War isn't Working* (21 August 1999) Dallas Morning News Online, Dallas TX. < www.dallas-news.com/>.

[iv] Greg Pierce, *Inside Politics*, Washington Times Online (26 August 1999) World News Communications, Washington, D.C. www.washtimes.com/politics/politics.html.

[v] Jacob Sullum, *Just a Cigar,* Intellectual Capital.com (12 August 19990 VoxCap.com, Washington, D.C.< www.intellectualcapitol.com/>.

[vi] Neil Innes, *How Sweet to be an Idiot* , Monty Python Instant CD Collection: Monty Python's Live at Drury Lane, (1994) Virgin Records Beverly Hills, CA.

[vii] *Cost of Raising a Child* Network for Family Life Education (March 1999) Family Life Matters Washington, D.C.

[viii] *Immigrants find success in Silicon Valley job* Associated Press (7 June 1999) Associated Press New York, NY.

[ix] *Tales from Hellmouth* (1999) <www.talesfromhellmouth.org>.

[x] Katie Merx *Schools, teachers get help: Kelly Services launches program to pair schools, substitute teachers in Metro Detroit* The Detroit News (26 October 1999) The Detroit News Detroit, MI.

[xi] Amy Beth Graves, *Ohio School Vouchers in Limbo* Foxnews.com(25 August 1999) Fox News New York, NY. www.foxnews.com.

xii Linda Dobson, *Rest in Peace, President Jefferson,* IntellectualCapital.com (19 August 1999) VoxCap.com, Washington, D.C. <www.intellectualcapitol.com/>.

xiii Alan Charles Kors and Harvey A. Silvergate *Shadow University* ([New York] Free Press 1998).

xiv *Minnesota school urges students and faculty to be fragrance free* Impact! Online (November 1994) Passport Educational Publishing MN.lrs.ed.uiuc.edu./impact/articles/perfume_ban/perfume_ban.ht ml>

xv *Britain Probes Organ Donation Report* Associated Press (6 July 1999) Associated Press New York, NY.

xvi Total number of 1998 tax returns filed by residents: 536,281 Single filers and some other categories less than $25,000 federal adjusted gross income: 221,377 Married filers less than $40,000 federal adjusted gross income: 108,596 Therefore adding both categories together, you have 329,973. Therefore dividing that number by the total number of resident tax returns filed in 1998, you have 62%. Data provided by State of Maine Revenue Services.

xvii" Rick Merrick ,*The U.S. Post Postal Service War on Private Mailboxes and Privacy q*

xviii James Carter, *What to Cut?* Investors Business Daily (17 August 1999), Los Angeles, CA.

xix Bruce Bartlett, *Taxes at Record Levels-Even with Tax Cut* Idea House (August 1999), National Center for Policy Analysis Washington D.C.www.ncpa.org.

xx David Hughes, Hamish MacDonell *Hague Savages Europe* Daily Mail (6 October 1999) Associated Newspapers Ltd. London UK.

xxi *Articles 2, 4 The North Atlantic Treaty,* (April 1999) NATO Brussels, Belgium.< www.nato.int/docu/basictxt/treaty.htm

xxii Jeremy Learning *School Board Bans Star of David necklace as possible gang symbol* The Freedom ForumOnline: Religion (18 August

1999) Freedom Forum Washington, D.C. <www.freedomforum.org/religion/1999/8/18gangwear.asp>

xxiii *Washington In Brief* Insight Magazine (6 September 1999) World News Communications Washington, D.C.

xxiv Howard Thompson, *Debunking the Myth of a "Christian" U.S* (1990) < alt.politics.libertarian>.

xxv for an explanation of English Deism go to www.utm.edu/research/iep/d/deismeng.htm.

xxvi *God Hates Fags.com* Westboro Baptist Church (1999) Topeka, Kansas.< www.godshatesfags.com>.

xxvii Antonio Mendoza *THE CULTS 'R US HIT LIST* (undated) <www.mayhem.net/Crime/cults1.html>.

xxviii *Violent Crime Sinks Since 94, study says, Lungren says 3 Strikes Making a Difference* Los Angeles Daily News (3 June 1998) UMI Company, Los Angeles, CA.

xxix *Harry Potter worries American Parents* (1 Oct 1999) World Entertainment News Network, Los Angeles, CA.

www.ingramcontent.com/pod-product-compliance
Lightning Source LLC
Chambersburg PA
CBHW031241280526
45784CB00004B/1666